CALICO CHRONICLE
Texas Women and Their Fashions
1830-1910

Betty J. Mills

Texas Tech Press
Lubbock, Texas, U.S.A.
1985

ISBN 0-89672-128-0 (paper)
ISBN 0-89672-129-9 (cloth)
Library of Congress Catalog Card Number: 84-52249
Texas Tech Press
Texas Tech University
Lubbock, Texas 79409
Copyright 1985 by Texas Tech University
Printed in the United States of America

To
The Museum
Texas Tech University

Wherein lies the kaleidoscope of
clues and clothes
that helped make this publication come about

and

In memory of my mother, Ivy G. Savage, a great
Texas lady and a pioneer in settlement, in education,
and in a woman's role of leadership

CONTENTS

FOREWORD

A never-dying optimism surely must have been an important virtue possessed by women who pioneered the early frontiers in America. There is no question that they had to "keep up or go under." Keeping up, both emotionally and physically, necessitated perseverance and hope.

How did these pioneer women dress—on the prairie, in the hill country, below the caprock, on the plateaus, in the timberland, around the bend of the Brazos? Were they indifferent to the clothes they wore?

While libraries are filled with accounts of the battles, Indian raids, land acquisition, and settlement of the west, little is recorded that verbally or visually documents what the women wore. There is good reason for this void. Examples of the inelegant dress of the people "who stuck it out" are extremely rare. Necessity and resourcefulness caused many of these garments to be worn out or converted into some other useful object.

Random clues do exist—in diaries, chronicles, reminiscences, biographies, portraits, and occasional photographs—that attest to the fact that even the women in desolate settings were concerned with what they wore and how they looked. They clung hopefully to a measure of calico and what it symbolized.

Once The Museum on the campus of Texas Tech University had launched its outdoor history interpretation as The Ranching Heritage Center in 1967, statewide interest in the program resulted in significant gifts of frontier dress, as well as tools and documents of early Texas history. It was in answer to repeated requests for assistance in interpreting the frontier lady's costumes and her role in clothing the family that this story was begun.

Although the setting has been confined to Texas in the text, historical documents witness the fact that settlers and their way of life were not so different from region to region. Nebraska was much like Oregon, New Mexico like Arizona. The degrees by which Texas developed made it distinctive. The development was a long, drawn-out process that encompassed a timespan from the early 1820s into the new century.

The title *Calico Chronicle* was chosen because of the significant position that calico held throughout most of the nineteenth century. Early settlers and homesteaders seldom made a supply list or record of purchases without including this plainly woven cotton fabric.

Calico had its origin in India in the fifteenth century as a fine luxury fabric named for its point of origin, Calicut, and originally was a fine white cotton cloth. Later, designs were painted on the fabric, then hand-printed. By the late eighteenth century the first calicoes printed in America were produced with engraved cylinders and were still expensive and much sought after fabrics in the early 1800s—so expensive that only the wealthy could afford them. Decades later, when production became more bountiful, calico remained in favor for its practicality, comfort, and beauty to the lady on the frontier, whether in Texas, on the high plains, or on the west coast. Its symbolism goes hand in hand with the frontier struggle for the badge of respectability, which was to make a decent appearance.

Development of the frontiers in Texas was clearly unique, in spite of its similarities to other regions. Barriers such as the Indian Territory, Mexico's rule and the struggle for independence from her, along with great geographic inaccessibility, were factors that delayed the movement across the state. While early colonization was in the Gulf Coastal region in and around San Antonio, farther inland the distances to supply sources were so great that settlement was slow. The establishment of military forts at scattered points served to offer re-enforcement for some adventuresome pioneers, but it was not until the railroad came onto the scene in the 1880s that movement began toward the north central part of the state and the plateaus below the caprock. By that time El Paso was attracting homesteaders from California. However, settlement on the South Plains and in so-called West Texas was almost two decades later. A brief resumé of the settlement of Texas, accompanied by maps, has been included to give the reader a review.

In no way is this treatise intended to be a detailed study of historical happenings; rather, an attempt has been made to set the stage—location and time—as a reflection of the movement of people into diverse parts of the state. Situations and time periods have dictated to a large extent the fashions to be found—fashions that in reality were a blending of the frontier functional, the saved-back-for-good, as well as the elegant and the beautiful. History has revealed that the love of beauty and the ornamental is innate in woman's nature, at best. At the very least, a woman of character, through all of Texas' formative years, was expected, as quoted from an 1865 issue of *Godey's Lady's Book and Magazine*, "to clothe herself respectably."

OFF TO TEXAS

THE CHALLENGE OF SETTLEMENT

In the saga of the old west, they came to Texas from wealthy plantations, from immigrant ships, from sophisticated cities, and from the penal colonies. They came to escape from the long arm of the law, from the disillusionment of an earlier failure, and for the challenge of a promising future. Texas—just the sound of it was appealing. It was the state whose name was taken from "Tejas," a league of Indian tribes, translated to mean friends or allies.

The conquistadors in the sixteenth century traveled to Texas in search of "glory, God, and gold." And later, people came from all walks of life in search of much of the same, but also for a new beginning. They came with degrees and pedigrees. They were literate and illiterate, and they came exercising their right to the pursuit of happiness, wealth, anonymity, escape, or power. This frontier was a magnet of promise. And people were off to Texas—"wild, boundless and free!" (Pickrell, 1970)—where land was available for the asking. How they arrived on this new frontier is a fascinating story and is important in tracing fashion. Ways of life, economics, and historic events that are reflected in dress weave a tapestry of the people of a given time.

PLANTING THE ROOTS

In 1821 a long, arduous trip by ship, rowboat, and finally dugout canoe brought the first group of Anglos, led by Stephen F. Austin, from New Orleans to a spot between the Brazos and the Colorado rivers. Austin instilled in his followers a faith in his vision of a Texas that offered eventual power and prosperity. These people stayed and built the first log cabin there. Settlers traveled by Gulf steamer and schooner, overland by wagon, on horseback, by stagecoach, or by riverboat for the many legs of their trip as they flowed into Texas. Many new arrivals came by ox cart or by barouche drawn by four fine horses (Fig. 1).

The road to Texas was seldom an easy one. In many cases the trip was made by degrees, with a stopover for several years to work and save enough money to continue the journey. One young couple who married in Kentucky in 1818 and headed toward Texas was forced to stop at Natchitoches Pass, Louisiana, where the husband operated a mercantile store for three years. It was 1821 before they were able to continue their journey and settle on the bank of the Brazos River in a one-room log cabin.

The lure of joining Austin's first colony brought young John Bunton from Tennessee by horseback. On his return to Tennessee for his bride, he persuaded a large group to join them in colonizing in Texas. This entourage of 140 people, including a large group of slaves, took passage down the Mississippi River to New Orleans where they boarded another steamer to cross the Gulf of Mexico. On this presumably passive trip, a Mexican man-of-war overcame them and took them by way of Vera Cruz to Mexico City where they were

FIG. 1.—Settlers came to Texas by riverboat and schooner and by covered wagon for "the last leg." (Reprint of original oil painting by Donald Teague, from the Harmsen Western Americana Collection.)

jailed. Several months later they were released to return to Tennessee. Undaunted, however, the John Bunton family made another attempt and they were able to reach Texas for settlement by 1840 (Pickrell, 1970).

The promise of cheap acreage kept a procession of land seekers pouring into the state during the 1840s. Wherever they landed, homesteaders craved neighbors and encouraged relatives and friends from the older states or homeland to join them. The feeling was well expressed by Peter Birk, a German immigrant who settled in the Texas hill country, in a letter to his family in Germany:

> Dear brothers and sisters, and friends: leave Germany and come here where you can live happily, well, and contentedly. If you work only half as much as in Germany, you can live without troubles and "put by" for the future.

Letters were filled with descriptions of living conditions, climate, availability of supplies, attractive features as well as the risks involved. Routes were recorded by travelers who had made the wearisome trip.

> You can go to Texas by land, through the states of Missouri and Arkansas, but this route is rough and tedious, and you will be likely to become discouraged before you arrive at the

most desirable part of the country. To go by water as far as Rodney, on the Mississippi River, and there take the Texas road . . . is a much more speedy and comfortable route . . . .

Those who are willing to risk the dangers of the ocean can have a still more speedy passage by going the whole route by water. [Fisher, 1940]

Although the majority of the people immigrating to Texas came from other American states, there also was a large and valuable immigration from European countries. One such couple was from Oldenburg, a state of the German Empire. Having lost their estate in Germany, this newly married couple set off on a nine-week voyage to New Orleans, Louisiana. There they joined with another family to charter a ship to Brazoria, Texas. The ship wrecked on the coast of Galveston Island, leaving them with no supplies; but they were finally able to make settlement at Cat Springs.

Despite the possibility of meeting hostile Indians, newcomers continued to move into this virgin land in a steady stream (Fig. 2). As a result, the frontier witnessed a blending of diverse cultural patterns and backgrounds that was clearly reflected in the mode of dress. Manners, customs, and heritage fathered in many states and European countries brought together a mixture of the crude and the cultivated that "ranged from the reliable roughness of buckskin to the refined elegance of broadcloth" (Hogan, 1947).

By 1849 Texas was securely a part of the United States, and was second only to California, which boasted vast gold discoveries, in attracting settlers. A year later Texas had five towns with a population exceeding 1,000 but none more than 5,000. The frontier continued to advance into Central Texas with a steady influx of covered wagons from Tennessee, Kentucky, Alabama—many of them crossing the Arkansas River at Little Rock. Colonies of German families moved in from the Indianapolis area, and groups of Quakers came from Ohio. Settlers were able to report favorably about the growth of the Tyler (Smith County) area:

This place 22 years ago, was in the woods with one or two log houses; now there is a population of two or three thousand, with about twenty five business houses, some of which sell one hundred thousand dollars worth a year for cash in gold and silver. [Chabot, 1940]

Trading posts followed in the shadow of military posts, and by the 1870s brave bands of settlers were moving into the area north and west of Fort Worth. People beyond Ohio seemed to colonize in groups, and during this time parties of Pennsylvania farmers came into areas such as Throckmorton County. The trading post that grew up around Fort Griffin, Albany, developed into a townsite. This became a pattern for small communities of people who had taken refuge near a fort.

Differences in dwelling structures resulted from regional varieties of materials as well as the diversity of settlers' backgrounds. Often the dwelling was dug out of the earth with a few logs secured above ground. In other regions, blocks were hewn from rock walls and massive stone structures appeared (Fig. 3). By the 1880s the vast plains, previously such a haven for the buffalo hunter, were being settled and broken into ranches, and the northern plains was becoming checkerboarded with farms. Lack of railroad

FIG. 2.—Leaving behind the familiar to face the unknown, families staked their claims from the Rio Grande to the Oklahoma Territory, from Louisiana to an undefined territorial boundary on the west. (Photograph from The Museum, Texas Tech University.)

FIG. 3.—Dwellings were constructed of materials native to the area, sometimes "bricked" out of the earth, as in this sodhouse. (Photograph from The Museum, Texas Tech University.)

routes held back settlement of the South Plains. This last frontier was finally being populated by the 1890s (Fig. 4).

Once lumber was being freighted by wagon from the railroad lines, simple box and strip houses were erected. These grew more comfortable and larger as time went by and as material became more readily available. It was 1909 when the railroad came onto the Llano Estacado at Lubbock, which made a supply route feasible and attracted many who had originally settled in East or Central Texas. Signs of development could be seen over most of the state at the beginning of the new century. Communities were flourishing all around, and before long elegant abodes were being constructed, and roots were firmly planted. Many homesteaders who had persevered were achieving a level of prosperity.

A WORLD OF CONTRAST

Many strong qualities characterized the women who began to appear in this world that was virtually untamed and still under the domination of Mexico. For those already attuned to hardship, life was simply a matter of shifting locations from one rural situation to another. Some had previously pioneered in Illinois, known as the Prairie State, and in Pennsylvania, Ohio, or the Indian Territory. Many came with religious sects and other groups, such as the predestinarian Baptists, the Quakers, and the Tennessee Whigs. There were child brides of fourteen or fifteen who came in support of a young man's dream. Also among them was the daughter of a well-to-do doctor from

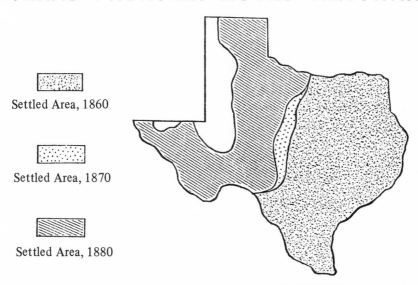

THE TEXAS NEWS, NOVEMBER 15, 1881

TEXAS FRONTIER MOVES WESTWARD

Settled Area, 1860

Settled Area, 1870

Settled Area, 1880

EXTENSION OF THE LINE OF SETTLEMENT

FIG. 4.—The expansion of frontiers in Texas was gradual and was spaced over a long interval of time. (Maps from *Texas News*, 1881.)

Morgan County, Alabama, a debutante from Baltimore, and the adopted daughter of a plantation owner in New Orleans. As the century progressed, some of the women who arrived included graduates of female seminaries, the daughter of the Chief Justice of the Supreme Court of Ireland, a young woman who was recently married to a doctor in Germany, and an accomplished French lady whose husband had been an artist in Paris. There were enterprising New Englanders and spirited countryfolk. They came from widespread points of the states—from Missouri, Tennessee, Kentucky, Indian Territory, Ohio, South Carolina, as well as immigrating from European beginnings—some humble, some "delicately trained."

One lady, it was said, brought to this young state the lavish hospitality and gracious social life of her homes in Philadelphia and Paris! The daughter of a French Creole who was a prominent cotton and sugar dealer in New Orleans came as a young bride. A French girl who married a native of Scotland moved from Tennessee to Louisiana, and finally landed in Beaumont, Texas, among the first settlers in the 1830s. The young daughter of an English family that was socially prominent enough for her presentation at Court to Queen Victoria changed her life-style from one of culture to a rugged life on a sheep ranch in Texas. A well-educated Norwegian woman, Elise Amalie Tvede Waerensk-jold, who married a man she met on the voyage to America, took a major role in the new state. The following was said about her:

> The lady of the aristocracy became a lady-jack-of-all-trades in her adopted country. She was recognized authority on land, cattle, grain, insects, prices, bankers, orchards, cotton, animals, wild and domestic, freed slaves, and weary willies! ... She learned to cope with grasshoppers, with blizzards, droughts, and floods, wind and weather of all kinds, such as tornadoes, thunder, lightning, hail, snow, ice and sleet. [Carrington, 1975]

Women came to Texas, and many of them remained, upholding the manners, language, enterprise, and valor that had distinguished their ancestors. The contrast of life-style between their previous world and current circumstance was often pronounced. Evidence of this heterogeneous citizenry in Texas in the early years is well reflected in the remnants of dress left to help record this story.

By whatever means a family traveled, packing for the move to Texas necessitated careful planning and discriminating choices. Not an isolated case was that of the Yoast family who left Virginia in the 1830s in style, riding in a carriage drawn by four prancing bays, wagons loaded with household goods, flax, a spinning wheel, table silver, and multiple slaves, guarded by two outriders. In Alabama they lost the first carriage. Because money was getting scarce, the trip was delayed three years while the husband ginned cotton and saved enough money to resume the journey. This time they left with a hack and the outriders in the wagons. When the hack gave way, the trip to Bastrop County, Texas, was finished in a covered wagon drawn by fourteen oxen. Bed and cooking pots were in the wagon with the riders (Pickrell, 1970).

Mary Ann Maverick, an early arrival on the Texas frontier, traveled in style, leaving South Carolina for Texas in a horse-drawn carriage; her party included "ten Negro slaves, a big Kentucky wagon, three extra saddle horses, and one blooded filly" (Brown, 1972). The wagon carried a tent, a supply of provisions and bedding, the cook, and the Maverick children. Another family "put out" for Texas from Alabama, with the family riding in a carryall drawn by a spanking team of horses, and a black driver in his accustomed seat. In the four wagons were the elegant clothes from the mansion, the silver, glassware, books of "culture," and the money in moneybags under all the goods in the wagons. Even the mahogany piano was loaded into a wagon for its eventual move into a log cabin.

These well-equipped entourages represent a minority of the immigrants moving onto this new vista. The majority were lucky to keep one wagon rolling, crowded as it was with all the earthly possessions they could fit into it. Almost always, space was allotted for a small trunk into which the family's best clothes had been carefully packed. Circumstances sometimes forced them to arrive with less than they started.

CLASSIC DRESS

THE EARLY YEARS

Getting to Texas was no small feat. Most families faced periods of hardship and deprivation. Long, arduous days of riding the wagon and miles of walking to lighten the wagon load, and cooking over open campfires, sometimes in the rain, took a great toll on the women and their wardrobes. Diaries refer to the fact that some of the travelers made little change in what they wore on the wagon train. One woman admitted that she started the trip with a dark woolen dress and wore the same one all the way until reaching destination. Sturdy aprons helped to protect the dress. Other women managed with one or two long full skirts with separate waists or jackets.

When camp was made for longer than overnight, and if water was available, the women heated up the wash pot and scrubbed clothes for the entire family, laying the garments out on the banks of the creek or on branches to dry. Washing by the full moon on occasion—even donning the clothes before completely dry—was not unusual. Long full skirts were the fashion, of course, but they also served to protect the legs and afford modesty. When a group of two or three full-skirted women gathered around in a circle, they provided a living shield for each other when privacy was needed.

While aprons and even petticoats sometimes had to be torn and used as bandages and to meet other emergencies, most women managed to guard the trunk that held the good dress. They were reluctant to sacrifice these symbols of another way of life and the hope of a promising future. Brambles that tore at the goods and tears from straining in action, along with honest wear, caused the women to get out the needle and thread and lay on patches and mend the worn and sometimes threadbare garments.

Occasionally a note crops up to reveal that some clothing construction was done while enroute. One woman with a merry outlook reported making a red calico frock in the wagon for wearing on the "nation's jubilee of liberty"—the Fourth of July. (Wherever they were, the travelers paused to rejoice on this great day.)

Because of the custom of silence in regard to mention of an expected baby, it was not unusual to find a few references in diaries to that hush-hush event. A gingham maternity gown was made by one lady from the cover on a feather bed. This she confided in her diary—but not orally.

Resourceful women sometimes gathered reed or bulrush at the riversides along the way and braided it into large sunshade hats to be tied on with the folded kerchief that they faithfully wore around the neck or carried in a pocket of the skirt. Before the Indians became hostile, there were occasions when the travelers bartered with them, trading an apron or some dry crackers for a pair of moccasins.

The trip, however, was always tedious and after so long a time of struggle and fatigue, it is understandable that there would be a lapse in the efforts to

Fig. 5.—The shelter of a tent was often the abode for the pioneers while the dugout or log cabin was being erected. (Photograph from The Museum, Texas Tech University.)

maintain a decent appearance. Still, when their final destination was becoming imminent, the women revived their awareness of neglect and were motivated to give attention to their hair and don the least shabby of the travel clothes in fulfillment of the great expected arrival.

When the audacious journey ended, all energies were consumed with settling for most of the newcomers. In many instances, the family did not immediately have a dwelling place until they could erect one, and when staking a claim they were miles from the nearest neighbor (Fig. 5). Little thought was given to what they wore.

Once necessities had been met, women, who were the shapers of the family began to crave and desperately need something suitable to wear. Clothing was necessary to lift the morale and strengthen the resolve. Some had to resort to buckskin for all members of the family, because it was most easily attainable. Buck deerskin was the lightest, most durable and pliable, and the Indians taught the settlers the best method of preparing it. Buckskin was especially suitable for the men and boys, but the women found it rather heavy for indoor work.

When no other goods were available the women are known to have cut up the drilling (heavy cotton twill that was used on the wagon trip) for dress material or to have made a dress from flour and feed sacks. One nostalgic story told of an isolated woman whose one dress became so shabby and had been mended so much that her husband traveled a dangerous 100 miles by horseback to reach a settlement with a store that had piece goods, where he was able to buy a length of calico for a dress for his wife. The trip was made over her protest, but the story describes well the importance of being properly clothed.

LINSEY-WOOLSEY

Having a loom and spinning wheel were luxuries not all families possessed, but most men had enough building skills to construct them, even though they might be crudely made. Commercially made ones were not available in Texas until the 1840s. Tools for making the cloth—the wheel for spinning the yarn and the loom for its weaving—were important to most families, as there was no nonsense about the need to supply the family with textiles. As soon as they could get the wool, cotton, or flax, women immediately set up their production.

A sturdy fabric would result from the combination of cotton or linen (derived from flax) used for a warp yarn in the loom and wool for the weft. This homespun fabric, referred to as linsey-woolsey or linsey-homespun, was considered by some to be coarse and ugly. It was, nevertheless, so important to the colonists that the woman of the house was reluctant to have anyone else cut into the goods. She felt more skilled at making use of every inch! It took almost two weeks of steady and earnest labor to spin enough thread for a dress, then another week to weave the fabric. Depending on the style and complication of construction, it could take an additional week to cut and stitch the garment, always by hand, as the sewing machine was not invented until 1846 and not generally in use in Texas until after the Civil War.

Preparing the fiber for the loom was a family affair. Even little children could help by picking the trash from the cotton and getting it ready for the older girls who kept the spinning wheel and loom humming a good part of every day. Daughters accepted willingly their role in helping produce the cloth.

> Six cuts of thread she must card and spin day by day or its equivalent in value in some other part of the cloth-making process . . . . Not only sheets, but blankets and cloth for her own undergarments and for the "homespun" dresses to be worn in this wilderness in the hope of saving the silk brought from old Kentucky. [Pickrell, 1970]

In some communities a common loom was shared by women who took turns weaving with their homespun yarn. One young widow wove cloth for her neighbors on her home loom or on the loom of her patrons, "taking many times in payment for her labor just as much corn as she could herself carry. . ." (Pickrell, 1970).

Dye for the yarn was made from all kinds of natural resources—weeds, moss, minerals of the earth, trees, berries, and nuts. Bark from the walnut, cedar, and butternut trees made a satisfactory brown. Actually, butternut could produce a range from gray to dark brown. Logwood made black; boiled sumac berries gave a warm red, as did madder. Peach and hickory bark, boiled onion skin, and copperas all furnished different shades of yellow. Purple came from oak and maple bark, and gray from cedar berries. Indigo, a popular blue dye made from a plant in India, was both expensive and difficult to obtain,

FIG. 6.—This linsey-woolsey homespun "heavy" dress of the 1840s was brought to Texas from Minnesota.

until it was discovered growing wild by the sides of the roads in Texas. Shades that resulted from these natural resources were not always predictable. Many women spoke of the "rich, pretty, soft colors as many as in Joseph's coat" (Carrington, 1975). One woman, however, admitted dyeing her woolen skirt with hickory bark each year with the result always being the "same ugly shade of brown."

Frocks made of homespun were often referred to as the "heavy dresses." The heavy dress shown in Fig. 6 is a linsey-woolsey homespun dyed deep indigo blue. It is made in the traditional one-piece style of plain, fitted bodice and full skirt that is pleated in front with fullness gauged in back and joined to the bodice with fine piping. The bodice is lined with coarse natural linen; the trim is two vertical bands of worn dark velvet ribbon framing the flat metal buttons down the front. Feelings about these heavy dresses are reflected in contemporary expressions of the early settlers:

> When the silk and velvets and laces she had brought with her became exhausted, when she was confronted with the necessity of wearing homespun dresses and russet shoes, her spirit rebelled. . . .
>
> Maris . . . put the women slaves to work in the house—spinning and weaving, carding, all the work, in short, incident to the manufacture of the ugly cotton and woolen cloth . . . saw a day coming when silk could not be had, either with money or with persuasion, and Maris preferred to use the cotton cloth in the hopes of preserving the precious silk.
>
> To take the silk out occasionally and let her slender fingers wander down the folds, just a few minutes at a time, a time snatched from her labor, to Maris this seemed a reinforcement of the desire in her heart to think always that she was a lady, no matter the circumstances surrounding that pioneer home. [Pickrell, 1970]

After wool production became relatively plentiful in Texas, an effort was made to produce silk. As early as 1835, according to the Nacogdoches police blotter, there was an unsuccessful attempt to propogate the silkworm in Texas. Accounts appear of repeated attempts in the 1840s and 50s to develop this industry, yet results were never satisfactory. So women had to content themselves with the linsey-woolsey, Texas calico, and an occasional piece of fine cotton muslin, imported silk or wool. Most of the women wore plain dresses they made—the style and perfection depending on their ability with the needle. "There were two widths in the skirt and a little waist and sleeve, that was all and that was our dress" (Ragsdale, 1976) is a fair description of the frocks worn by many of the women. Surviving garments of linsey-woolsey are scarce, but the tobacco brown frock shown in Fig. 7 illustrates well the distinctive beauty that could be attained with this "homely" fabric. The dress was originally made in Germany and brought to Texas by a family who homesteaded in Colorado County. While the general look of the dress is in tune with features of the 1830s, construction techniques indicate that it could not have been made earlier than the mid-1840s. The bodice displays fan-pleated folds from the shoulders, meeting in the center front at the waistband. This drapery is arranged onto a tight-fitting lining of coarse natural linen; the front and back are then sewn together at the shoulder seam set toward the back. Seams are strongly backstitched and edges are overcast. The bodice

FIG. 7.—This shadow plaid dress in the style of the 1840s was brought from Germany to the Hill Country in the 1870s. The shawl, a fine Paisley of the type woven in Scotland, was used in Indiana before its owner brought it to Texas.

opens down the center front to the waistband, fastening with hooks and eyes of flattened brass wire, then opens into the skirt on the left front seam. A generous, brown cambric pocket is inserted in the right side front seam, and the skirt is gauged onto the waistband. Gauging is a method, then and now, of gathering large amounts of cloth into a small area. A series of running stitches is made, large on the wrong side and very small on the right side, one row above the other. With the fullness drawn up to the required size, the gathers are stitched on by taking a small stitch into the outside of each fold. The effect is that of precise, even, minute pleats with an overall appearance of having been stroked into place.

The skirt of this brown linsey dress is faced on the lower edge with brown silesia, then edged with wool braid, a practice that did not begin until the 1840s. The sleeves are lined with coarse natural linen joined to a piece of faded blue plaid gingham—evidence that the woman who fashioned the dress resourcefully used what was at hand. Multiple patches on this frock tell a story of extensive wear; yet the fabric remains strong.

The general look of the dress is sturdy, the color drab, but trimmed with a handmade lace collar and brooch, it becomes a lady's good dress, and therefore was saved back to survive for its place in The Museum Collection.

TEXAS CALICO

Inasmuch as most of the settlers had little money to spend, and expendable things were used up or worn out, they were challenged with the task of finding sewing goods they could afford. Availability and high prices were so significant that the fact was recorded in correspondence from early settlers:

> Once in a great while we are able to obtain a small piece of unbleached domestic, or a bit of calico, at the exorbitant price of seventy-five cents a yard, from someone passing through the country, but this is very seldom. The common dress of the man and children is made of buckskin, and even the women are often forced to wear the same. [Dewees, 1968]

The length of time they had been in Texas was strongly reflected in their dress. Mrs. Henry Ray confided to a friend in Virginia in a letter she wrote about 1830:

> Acting on my mother's advice, I brought clothes enough to last us several years; others have done the same, but the great majority have brought scanty wardrobes. The question of buying dry goods here is a serious one. Calico costs seventy-five cents per yard! As money is scarce with us all, a lady seldom has more than one Texas calico dress. [Pennybacker, 1888]

Calico, a plain cotton printed fabric, played an important role in clothing the families on the frontiers. It was desired for its beauty as well as its practicality. While in the early years of the nineteenth century the price of calico remained high, in time America was exporting rather than importing it, and calico goods for over a century enjoyed a popularity that fluctuated from one that was exclusive and attainable only by the elite to a position of favor because of availability at a low price. Somber at first, these printed goods took on a whole new range of bright and strident colors after the introduction of coal tar dyes in 1856 (American Fabrics Magazine, 1960). Although the first cotton was exported from Texas in the 1830s from the Stephen F. Austin Colony, the term "Texas calico" did not mean that the fabric was manufactured in the state, rather that is was procured from a source in Texas.

How a woman got her "one Texas calico" was not uncommonly like that found in an account of "Folk Life in Early Texas," written some time in the 1830s. Several families would join together once or twice a year to send to market for supplies. For family members remaining behind, the return of the buying party was a major event. On the fixed day of the buying party's arrival, people came together for division of the merchandise. Its dispersal went something like this: To D. Davis, 20 pounds flour, 20 pounds sugar, 20 yards domestic, 1 bolt of calico . . . (Carrow, 1947). Who made the selection of the calico is an interesting question. Naturally, the choice fell to the lot of the men on the supply wagon, but so welcome was this treasure that a woman accepted it, regardless of color or pattern. One fact was made clear: the wardrobes for most families were slim, even meager: "We had few dresses, maybe a calico for nice, but never more than one nice dress and one or two of the heavy dresses" (Pickrell, 1970). That calico dress cost about the same as a silk dress later in the century. During the Civil War, calico of the commonest kind reportedly cost from $4.00 to $5.00 per yard (Steen, 1955). By 1872 it was very cheap in San Antonio—"25 yards to the dollar, and merchants used it in place of brown paper for wrapping purposes." Calico, which occupied an important role for frontier families, fluctuated somewhat in price according to its quality and to the location at which it was purchased.

Early Milam settlers met the schooner or steamboat nearest Brazosport, over 160 miles away, for supplies from New Orleans. Later, provisions were brought on horseback from Natchitoches, which was 300 miles away. Even so, many women lamented that there was "not a yard of cloth to be bought nearer than New Orleans and transportation was slow and uncertain" (Walker, 1944).

By 1837 Houston was a village of 100 log and frame houses. It was also an important, although limited, supply source. One merchant recounted that in 1844 he had the misfortune of having his merchandise all washed overboard in transit but was able to retrieve at least one bolt of red calico that had been thoroughly wet. This he retailed for one dollar a yard—and the women were glad to pay the price. A "store" in Dallas at this same time consisted of a barrel of whiskey and 3 bolts of calico. Calico could be purchased there at fifty cents per yard. The first real mercantile store in Dallas was not opened until 1846 (Greene, 1973).

A decade later a German immigrant wrote home:

> Clothes are not so expensive as one imagines in Europe. Calico cloth is coarse and comes in dull patterns, priced at fifteen to twenty cents per yard, which is not unreasonable, but if a better quality were available they would in the end not wear it anyhow. [Ragsdale, 1976]

By the late 1850s Americans were consuming more calico than any other people in the world. From *Peterson's Ladies International Magazine* for

Fig. 8.—Sometimes a family ordered a full bolt of calico to outfit most members of the family. (Photograph courtesy of Montgomery Ward & Co.)

August 1876 came this claim: "Even a calico dress can be made to look stylish; and one made after this model cannot fail to do so." Calico was a fabric that they could afford. The outcome of its use was a varied pageant of costume. Families bought a full bolt at one time and made matching garments for members of the family (Fig. 8). The story is told of a Baptist preacher seeing his wife and children fingering a red calico in the mercantile. He asked the clerk how much was on the bolt. "Twenty yards," replied the clerk. Forthwith, the preacher announced, "I'll take it all," and he picked up the bolt and carried it to the wagon.

The Museum Collection includes a calico bodice from the late 1830s which is all that remains of a dress that may have been recycled for another use. This cotton bodice is printed with an overall pattern of vines and branches in black and white on light tan background. All the bodice seams are piped with ⅛″ string cord, covered with black cotton goods. The slightly raised waistline has a narrow self-belt set-in with black piping on each side. The unfinished seam on the bottom of the belt indicates it was joined to a skirt at some time. The bodice opens up the front to a plain round neck and is secured only at the waist with flattened brass wire hooks and eyes. The coarse cotton lining fastens snugly with multiple hooks and eyes. The sleeves are very low-set and puffed at the elbow, extending over the hand with a turned-back cuff that is also piped around the edge. Most assuredly there was at one point a matching skirt attached to this bodice brought to Texas from Ohio by the Baird family.

In spite of the fact that many of the women owned fashionable European modes and admired the stylish dress, they were flexible in practice and resorted to a pragmatic approach for everyday wear. They often adopted "home knitted stockings, plain loose blouse or jacket and a gathered long skirt" (Ragsdale, 1976). This style indicates a carry-over from the very functional "shortgown" that predominated among the colonists in rural Pennsylvania and surrounding states from the last half of the eighteenth century. It was basically a homespun linen worn over a linsey-woolsey petticoat. For want of more updated patterns to follow, and because of the ease of construction and comfort in wearing, this two-piece style was one favored by women in the years during and after The Republic (Fig. 9). A chronicler commented, on visiting one lady, that she was "clad in a well-fitting gown—of course it fitted well, for she had made it herself, the material being 'lindsay', or once in a while, gaily printed calico bought at ruinous prices from some peddler happening to stray her way" (Pickrell, 1970).

While sketches and portraits are a lead to the style of dress worn, they offer no information about sewing techniques, which can only be found from inspecting original examples of clothing. Based on detailed studies of dresses worn by women on the frontier, some of the features that appeared consistently in the one-piece classic style of dress of the second quarter of the nineteenth century will be examined.

FIG. 9.—The shortgown shown in *The Pioneer Cowpen*, by Richard Petri, depicts the style adopted by women in Texas. (Courtesy of Janette Long Fish.)

The Genteel Dress

Throughout the early periods of settlement, the majority of women retained an interest in any new style, in spite of their circumstances. The frontier was desolate and lonely, and the women craved for a look at what the fashionable lady was wearing. Letters sent back home often made mention of a visitor handsomely dressed in costumes by city dressmakers. An example of such a dress is the sheer, green and white striped muslin shown in Fig. 10. It features the fully lined gigot or leg-of-mutton sleeves and a full skirt gauged carefully to the bodice. The lappet weave gives an embroidered look to this fine cotton made in European style of 1830.

A famous port for foreign goods, New Orleans was considered the "Paris of America" to Texas folks. Mary Austin Holley, who was introduced to the mode set in England and France, brought that influence with her when she came from her plantation home in Louisiana to visit Austin's Colony in 1830. Fine, light cotton, expensive and highly esteemed, was the privilege of the elite in the early nineteenth century. Even as it became more attainable, elegant light-colored cotton was still reserved for the well-to-do, carrying with it the connotation of belonging to the leisure class.

The dress shown in Fig. 10 has all the features of styles from the 1830s. Fine piping is corded around the neckline, the seams of the sleeves, and the basque, which fastens down the center back with flattened brass wire hooks and eyes. The sleeves are exaggerated, full gigot or leg-of-mutton. The ankle-length skirt, attached to the bodice with gauging, is finished around the lower edge with a false hem (a common practice used to give the effect of a deep hem without the use of so much of the expensive cotton goods). A wide hem added weight to the lower skirt edge and caused it to billow out over the multiple petticoats. A false hem was created by using a wide facing turned under and hemmed to the inside of the skirt.

Had this fine cotton dress not been saved back for good, it probably would have been remodeled, cut down for a child, or fashioned into an apron or some other useful item. Certainly this would have been the case if the lady had ventured deeper into the frontier where supplies were difficult to obtain.

"A Visit to Texas, with Notes on That Country by a Lady" was written on foolscap with quill in 1831 by Mary Austin Holley. This treatise, finally titled *Texas. Observations, Historical, Geographical and Descriptive*, was the outcome of her visit to Austin's Colony with a view to permanent settlement, and includes her observations on fashions in the community. Mary Austin Holley was definitely fashion conscious, having been taught sewing, knitting, embroidery, and drawing when she was a young girl back East. As the adopted daughter of a dry goods merchant, she had access to a wide selection of fine fabrics and had learned to design and make suitable clothes for herself. The presence of this genteel lady in the colony was a refreshing diversion for the women and it gave them the opportunity to hear news from the city.

FIG. 10.—A classic example of 1830s fashion. The bonnet of silk and wool Maltese bobbin lace is referred to as a "bibi" bonnet.

Commenting on the dress of the inhabitants of Austin's Colony, Mrs. Holley observed: "a taste of luxury displayed by females in the article of dress which would compare with that of old settlements of our country." She further observed:

> No new country in America presents a population more tasteful and genteel in dress than Texas; and one would suppose, on visiting a ball-room or a place of fashionable resort—for such there are—that he had fallen among the elite of a flourishing and refined community; when the fact is, he would be among the common class of a country where there are no distinctions, where rich and poor blend together, and where all are able to, and on occasions present the same genteel appearance. [Holley, 1836]

The so-called fashionable women did not appear just in resort situations. In many instances, women had brought with them fragments of their previous way of life. About 1830 one young Virginia beauty brought her buff-colored velvet ball gown with her when she settled in Bastrop County. It was described in this manner:

> The skirt measuring yards and yards around the bottom but escaping the floor by an inch, the bodice plain and tight, the sleeves puffed to astonishing proportions, a lace bertha of exquisite design. [Pickrell, 1970]

Through the years she would don this elegant gown for wearing to community dances, even though the setting was crude. The necklace of amethyst and pearls, her high standing comb, amethyst and pearl earrings and matching bracelets came out on these special occasions. Women often sacrificed a pair of satin slippers (usually homemade) as they danced and danced on the dirt floor with dust rising from the stomp of happy feet.

By far the most popular style of dress, however, was the uncluttered, functional long skirt "fulled onto the waist." The waist was a simple-fitted bodice that opened up the front and was finished with a round neck, left plain, or decorated with a collar or brooch. Patterns were often copied from an existing frock—unpicked or taken apart—and used as a guide. Cotton in stripes, checks, plaids, small prints, or plain colors, and woolens in varying qualities, or in combination with cotton, were the fabrics most often used.

Favorite colors were tender brown, olive, amber, vanilla, and grayed delicate tones. An early classic genteel frontier dress in sheer beige, light-weight wool woven with vertical flecks of brown, and the surface decorated with small, dark brown woven rectangles, is shown in Fig. 11. The stitching is not fine, but it is durable and was made probably some time during the 1830s and worn in Austin, Texas. The fine quality of fabric indicates that this was a "good" dress, probably a barège, a light-weight wool often spoken of with reverence in memoirs. Although the bodice fits loosely, this sheer wool dress has a fitted lining of two kinds of fabric—a brown print for the back and a coarse white cotton for the front, illustrated in the closeup of Fig. 11. Shanked, brown china buttons decorate the front opening of the bodice, with no visible means of fastening. The darted, fitted lining fastens snugly with white china buttons and buttonholes. The long, full balloon sleeves, puffed at the dropped shoulderline, as well as at the cuffs, are fully lined with a lavender printed cotton fabric.

The skirt, comprised of six lengths of 22 inch material, gauged onto the waistband, has a capacious pocket, over nine inches long and three and one-half inches wide, inserted in the right front side seam. This clever device for providing a place to carry a handkerchief, keys, sewing tools, even a tiny drawstring bag, was initiated about the 1830s when the skirts were becoming very full. The pocket was entirely concealed in the seam, and almost all dresses had one. The lower skirt edge is turned under and extended with lavender printed cotton to make a three-inch false hem.

Stitching on this garment is not fine, but the white pelerine (collar) exhibits a remarkable degree of fine white work—white embroidery on sheer white muslin. A meticulous chainstitch, made with a tambour hook, outlines the designs. Drawnwork filling stitches and buttonholed scallops are all worked with a needle (Fig. 12). The "morning cap" in Fig. 11 bears fine embroidery and skilled hand sewing. The wearing of the white pelerine and sheer, embroidered, starched white cap is a fashion from the early 1800s that did not decline until the 1850s. In 1857 young married ladies were advised that they "need not wear caps until they had acquired the endearing name of 'mother'" (Cunnington, *et al.*, 1976).

FRONTIER CLASSIC

Whether of homespun, calico, or silk, a classic style dress dominated women's fashion for a good part of the nineteenth century. In the early years this classic style dress was called the "round dress," a term indicating a dress with joined bodice and skirt without a train. The skirt was closed all around, that is, not open in front to expose an underskirt, as in the eighteenth century. The bodice was snugly fitted by subtly shaped darts or concentrated gathers in both center front and back. The shoulder seam sloped toward the back, and the armscye was very low off the shoulders.

This standard style, well represented in the dress shown in Fig. 13, is constructed of fine buff-colored muslin, printed with trailing small floral pattern of fern green, claret red, and lavender on black vines. The long, full sleeves are gathered and piped into the armscyes which drop low off the shoulders and are finished with a narrow selvage-edged triple ruffle gathered into the wrist. Made over a fitted lining of coarse cotton twill, the waist has fullness drawn to the waistband at the center back and center front where it fastens with white china buttons up to the high, round neck. Piping trims the waistband where the wide skirt (146 inch circumference) is finely gauged as it is joined to the bodice, shown in the closeup of Fig. 13. The lower skirt edge is trimmed with three graduated tucks above the 4 inch hem and then bound with narrow cotton twill binding. A long tubular pocket is inserted in the right front seam. This pretty and delicate frock, made of muslin typical of the early 1830s, was worn for such a long time that the bodice had to be totally

FIG. 11—A "genteel" dress made of sheer beige barège. A variety of goods was used for construction of the lining.

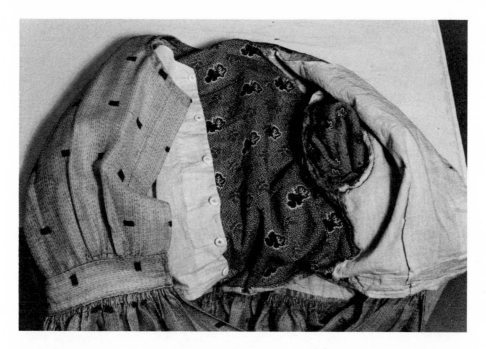

underlined by Museum conservators. Certain features of this dress indicate a
late 1830s style, although the tucks and the binding on the lower skirt edge
are associated more with the 1840s. Faded and worn though this frock is, its
classic beauty and simplicity cannot be denied. The lady who brought this
dress from Illinois to Texas evidently found it hard to relinquish for other
uses.

Another typical frock with an almost timeless appeal is the one shown in
Fig. 14, worn in the southern part of the state by a lady who came from
Germany to settle in Weimar, located between Houston and San Antonio.
Made of fine beige cotton calico sprigged with tiny brown and turkey red
floral designs, the dress has rounded, full shoulders outlined with fine piping
(1/16 inch cording covered with fabric of the dress) where the sleeves are set
in low to a dropped shoulderline. The skirt, five lengths of material tediously
gauged onto the fitted waistband, is finished with a heavy cording around the
lower edge. Self-ruching trims the high round neck, the front opening, and the
sleeve edges. The ever-present "bag" pocket is hidden in a side seam on the
right.

This style was so popular that later generations often commented that
grandmother's dresses were all made from the same basic pattern—five yards
around and gathered as full as could be into the waistband (Carrington, 1975).
Although from the mid-1840s on many dresses were made in two pieces, they
had the look of a one-piece dress. The photograph file of The Museum, Texas
Tech University, documents the universality of this style (Fig. 15). A dress with

FIG. 12.—The degree of excellence achieved by the women in the 19th century in their needlework is shown in this detail of whitework on the pelerine collar.

plain skirt, full body and trimmed sleeves was said to require ten yards of calico. The same thing made up in silk "for an ordinary-sized person" would require fourteen yards, because silk was usually of narrower width than cotton, twenty to twenty-two inches wide. Examples in The Museum Collection are made up in varieties of material, such as calico, printed cotton, dimity, wool challis, silk plaid, grosgrain striped silk taffeta, and muslin.

A stylistic variation of this period is the classic-looking model shown in Fig. 16. The fabric is fine forest green wool challis printed with chevron pattern of black on a pale green stripe. The dress blends features of the 1830s with those of the 1840s: a waistband joining the bodice to the long, full skirt which sweeps the floor where it is finished with cambric false hem or facing. Wool braid is stitched around the lower edge. The bodice shaping retains the diagonal lines from shoulder to center waist with gathers, rather than the fan pleating found in the brown linsey-woolsey (Fig. 7). The modified balloon sleeves, which is a style carried over from the 1830s, are lined with a printed beige cotton and set into the very low shoulderline with piping. The pristine high round neck was adopted in the 1840s, as indicated in *Godey's Lady's Book*, newly published authority on what women's styles would be:

> ... to be introduced this winter, made up to the throat, with three rows of buttons down the front, and the sleeves cut like those of a man's coat. A small round cambric collar double, not two collars, but the two sides of the one stitched together and made very stiff, with or without a narrow Valenciennes round, will be worn with these dresses.

FIG. 13.—Printed muslin dress is made up in a style that for many years was a classic on the frontier. The technique of gauging the skirt and attaching it to the bodice is shown in the closeup.

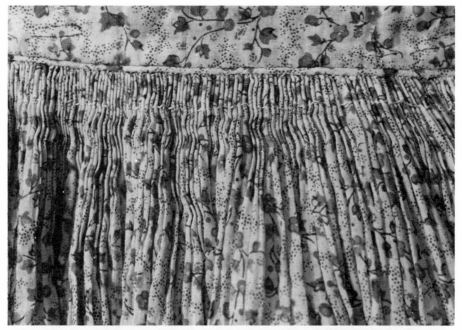

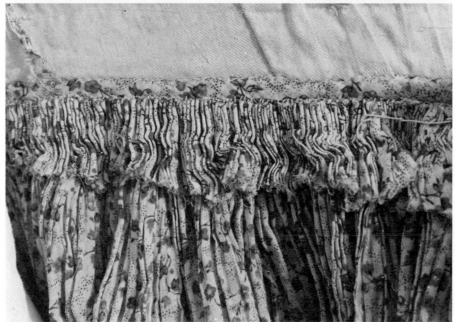

FIG. 14.—This handmade frock of sprigged beige calico is a typical mid-century fashion. The straw shepherdess bonnet has its own bonnet basket. The Paisley shawl of the 1850s was a wrap reserved for special occasions.

Only under close inspection is it obvious that this green challis dress was remodeled from an earlier period. A carefully matched extension has been made to the bottom of the bodice. Its lining of muslin does not extend all the way to the waistband, although it is stitched into the side seams and buttons snugly over the bust. The length of the lining and the extension of the bodice indicate that the dress originally had a raised waistline, which was fashionable through most of the 1830s. Stitching lines and other visible clues of alteration attest to skillful workmanship. Records show that this frock was worn by a lady in Dublin, Texas.

Several techniques of construction were consistently observed in the examples of early frontier dresses cited here. Whether of necessity or a sense of prudence and economy, in each case the seams were very narrow, only wide enough to catch the selvage. While a wide hem gave weight and quality to the full skirt, a false hem gave the same effect and saved a decided measure of goods. The dressmaker made the most of every square inch, oftentimes extending the waistband on the bodice with small pieces of fabric.

Of the dresses inspected, the lining was repeatedly found only in the bodice and sleeves, frequently exhibiting use of a variety of fabrics, which demonstrates another move for economy's sake. Few of the front opening bodices had visible means of fastening, even though the lining was made to fasten securely. All examples had the long tubular "bag" pocket concealed in the side seam. Corded piping, a sewing technique begun in the 1820s designed to strengthen and outline the seams, appears in every bodice in varying degrees of usage.

Even though skirts dropped from ankle to floor-length in the late 1830s, they grew longer by mid-century, with added length in the back to trail on the floor; thus, there was a need for binding the lower edge with braid for protection. A letter written from Austin in 1851 includes this observation:

> Have you adopted the American Costume yet? Augusta writes me she wears it, and I have been trying to persuade Caroline to come out in it here and make a sensation. We have not seen it yet, but Carry is very partial to very long skirts. [Hart and Kemp, 1974]

Unquestionably, a large populace of the newcomers arrived with very little clothing, some with nothing more than that which they wore upon their arrival. European immigrants often retained a strong influence from their homeland in their dress. This was partly of necessity, but it also served to form a bond with their kin who followed at a later date. By the 1840s and 50s, the Polish and the Germans were forming strongholds just up from the coast toward San Antonio and in the hill country. Their styles, for the most part, were distinctively European. As the century progressed and replacements were necessary, their garments began to follow the trend around them, retaining echoes of the classic style of frontier dress.

The much-patched, sturdy, gray one-piece dress shown in Fig. 17 was made as late as the 1880s. The coarsely woven fabric resembles flannel, in feel, and was originally trimmed with olive green wool braid. Except for being all

FIG. 15.—These unidentified women are wearing one of the styles that was a favorite from 1840 through the 1860s. The full, gathered skirt and fitted basque button up the front to a tiny collar; the sleeves are inset to a dropped shoulderline.

FIG. 16.—Striped wool challis dress, originally made in the style of the 1830s, was worn in Dublin, Texas, in mid-century.

machine stitched, its style, with the inset belt, reflects the period of the 1840s with less fullness in the skirt. Signs of hard usage are evident by the presence of a dark gray knitted patch on the skirt, a striped light gray patch on the sleeve, and the fragments of trim. It was worn in the Texas hill country by a German immigrant.

Until after the Civil War most of the women in the settled parts of Texas continued to follow the style of the long, full skirt, which was either attached to or made separate from the bodice. Little diversity is obvious in the basic style—whether the homely linsey, the heavy dress, the good calico, or the silk visiting dress. The major difference is in the degree and type of trim and the extravagance in the usage of material. Underpinnings also made a difference, as fancy dress, like the two-piece cobalt blue silk shown in Fig. 18, always was worn over hoops and/or crinolines.

Once the deprivation that accompanied wartime was past and the railroad was infiltrating the state, it was no longer necessary or prudent to spend time with hand weaving. Yard goods were increasingly available at village mercantiles, the sutler's at the fort, or through mail order.

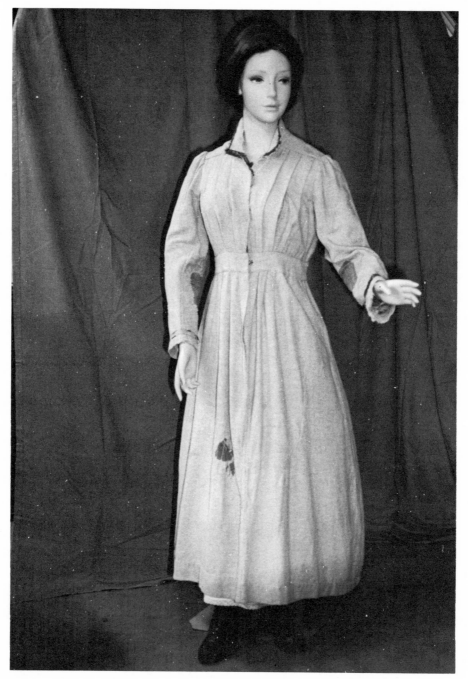

Fɪɢ. 17.—This gray dress of coarsely woven cotton shows signs of hard usage.

FIG. 18.—Many women in Texas owned elegant gowns such as this one in the late 1860s.

FRONTIER SIGNATURES

While the plainly styled one-piece frock appeared throughout at least two-thirds of the nineteenth century, there were other distinctive marks of dress that distinguished women on the frontier; Texas was no exception. Anonymous as they might appear, those frontier signatures abounded wherever there was settlement. They included particularly the shawl, the bonnet, and the apron. For many pioneer women, the shawl and the apron added the only touch of decoration to an otherwise plain ensemble.

THE SHAWL

The fashion of wearing a shawl or cape began in the 1830s when the massive sleeves made a fitted wrap almost impossible to wear. Although the sleeves slimmed down by the 1840s, the shawls and capes had so ingratiated themselves that they continued to be favored for many years. Women enjoyed wearing the shawl because it was easily handled over the large bell skirts, and it was available in a variety of materials, such as cashmere, Paisley, printed silk, embroidered China silk, Shetland wool, lace, and others.

During a good part of the nineteenth century, owning a "Paisley" was the epitome of elegance. This was a shawl of great beauty patterned after the earlier and fine handwoven Kashmir shawls from India. In the early 1800s the Scottish and English learned to produce these shawls on a draw or jacquard loom and called them "Imitation India Shawls." They sold the shawls at a fraction of the cost of the earlier handwoven ones, and soon Paisley, Scotland, had cornered the market.

Many of these fine shawls, bearing the Indian pine cone design in rich hues woven around a black center, made the voyage from the Old Country with the immigrants to the new states. The ones most frequently found in Texas were woven in Paisley, Scotland, or Norwich, England. In time, merchants were importing "Paisleys," and they were available for purchase in some Texas emporiums. Even when they were falling out of favor in the 1880s, the $500 shawl was being offered from Lord & Taylor for $275! Obviously, a shawl of this quality represented an important family purchase. The Paisley shawl in Fig. 14 is shown over a classic tan calico dress which, teamed with the little straw bonnet, made the lady who wore it in the 1850s dressed up in what was probably her best outfit.

Godey's Lady's Book at this time cautioned ladies thusly: "The fashion of appearing in the street without a scarf, shawl, or mantilla is not considered ladylike, nor is it the fashion" (Payne, 1965). Some shawls, of course, were more utilitarian than decorative. In 1865, *Godey's Lady's Book* advertised crocheted shawls to be ordered by mail at prices ranging from $9 to $30. Plain shawls were only $4. By the 1870s a Josephine (blush-colored) stripe shawl could be had for $2 from Montgomery Ward & Co., and an extra-heavy double plaid cost $3.50. Because double plaid shawls were very large,

FIG. 19.—Quaker bonnet of black sateen and shawl of gray twilled silk were worn by a Quaker woman preacher in the 1870s and were brought onto the Llano Estacado in the 1880s.

FIG. 20.—An ordinary, everyday shawl of fringed black wool is shown here with a handmade bonnet of lavender printed calico.

FIG. 21.—This brown calico skirt is comprised of several lengths of goods gathered onto a waistband and is worn with a white muslin blouse. The bonnet of fine, sheer wool was made about 1860 and brought to Texas from Georgia soon after the Civil War. The fringed fascinator is crocheted in the shell stitch and dates about 1865.

FIG. 22.—The versatile triangular shawl, known as a fascinator, served double duty as a headcovering in this picnic scene in Motley County in the 1880s.

measuring 63 x 126 inches, some might eventually be made into a dress by an ingenious woman who had no other resource for fabric.

Examples of shawls, many testifying to a life of hard use, have survived the years and remain to illustrate the wide variety of choice available to the women who wore them. Some of these shawls are nothing more than a large square of wool or silk, fringed and folded into a triangle (Figs. 19, 20). There are coarse homespun shawls of somber shades, plaid wools of varying hues, fine striped ottoman, imitation camel's hair, and numerous crocheted and knitted ones. It was even possible to order a wide selection of ready-made, hand-crocheted shawls at a very low price soon after the Civil War.

Brown, drab mourning shawls were widely worn. Those made of fine black wool and silk, trimmed with macramé fringe, were some of the prettiest ones. The Broché was a shawl of great beauty woven of heavy fabric with a raised design. One young girl recorded the special event of Papa's bringing a Broché shawl to Mama when he returned to Fort Griffin, Texas, from a trip to Santa Fe, New Mexico, in the 1860s. A shawl of this quality cost as much as $25.

A hand-crocheted, triangular shawl, known as a fascinator, which blithely belied its name, was another favorite wrap that appeared in the wardrobe of almost every lady and young girl on the frontier. This versatile, light-weight woolen covering was the most practical of headwear; it could also be draped around the shoulders as a shawl (Figs. 21, 22). By the latter part of the nineteenth century, handmade fascinators worked in a shell stitch of Shetland floss could be bought ready-made for as little as twenty cents. Many of them were fashioned from left-over yarn; others represented a labor of love, perhaps a Christmas present. There also was the "Cloud," a loosely knitted, oblong shawl of fine mohair yarn, usually in white or delicate colors, illustrated earlier in Fig. 6.

THE BONNET

The most distinctive badge of frontier dress, and certainly the most conspicuous, is the bonnet. All nonsense aside, the bonnet represented an anonymous statement of dedication and purpose.

While the bonnet was a style of hat adopted early in the nineteenth century, beginning as a large straw hat tied on the head with a scarf, it fell to the pioneer women to convert it into a practical form for everyday wear. This was accomplished with the sunbonnet. The Victorian period produced a multitude of bonnet styles—many elegant and fancifully trimmed—that played a role in the frontier woman's life. The sunbonnet, the mainstay of everyday wear, is most often remembered. Seldom did the pioneer woman leave the house without tying on a bonnet. When she did, it was often with regret, as observed by Mrs. Sinks in 1840:

> Instead of acting with the usual good sense of frontier people, wearing sunbonnets, . . . we donned little riding caps. We were not exactly roasted when we came back, but we brought with us a resplendent set of faces. [Reid, 1942]

Bonnets were the most universally used of all homemade garments except dresses. Sunbonnets, of course, held the lead. Guided by imagination, material available, influence of her associates, and exposure to current style, the pioneer women often came up with interesting creations, many of them bearing a peculiar charm. In her autobiography, Mrs. Barr (1913) described the white sunbonnets of the Texas girls as things of beauty; the very act of their removal communicated "a pleasant surprise and revelation of unsuspected charm."

Accounts of fancy bonnets found on the frontier include that of the promenade costumes observed in Houston in the early 1840s. The writer commented on one that could have been lifted "out of the pages of *Godey's*." It was a bonnet of pink satin with a crown towering three or four inches above the face, much in the fashion of the bobbin lace bonnet (Fig. 23). Inside, under the brim, was a double ruching of tulle with minute bows of satin and sprigs of flowers. Fastened to the crown was a veil about a yard wide and more than a yard and a quarter long, "elaborately wrought in white flowers and finished at the lower edge with a rich border," it was hardly the type of headgear that one would expect to find in an outlying frontier settlement (Reid, 1942).

Later in the 1840s, as the size of bonnets began to shrink, they were shaped over the crown of the head, creating an elongated brim. The printed lavender calico shown in Fig. 24 exhibits the everyday style. Fabric is shirred on rows of stiffened cording. The crisp, fresh condition of the calico used for this bonnet tells of the quality of early cotton fabrics. Straw bonnets for dress also

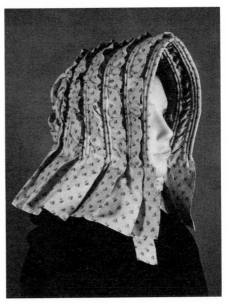

Fig. 23.—This "Bibi" bonnet (1830) is made of finely corded cream silk, with crown, bavolet, and brim ruffles of handmade Maltese bobbin lace of silk and wool.

Fig. 24.—Closeup of lavender calico bonnet (1840-1850) shown also in Fig. 20. Shirring is accomplished over stiffened cording.

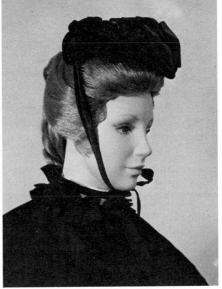

Fig. 25.—This natural plaited open straw bonnet (1840-1850) is one of the numerous varieties of headgear fashionable in early Victorian times.

Fig. 26.—A good black bonnet like this one (1860-1870), made of velvet and satin, often served a lady for several decades.

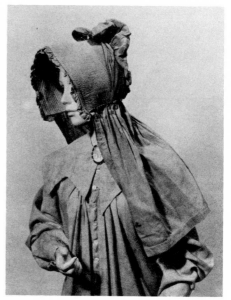

FIG. 27.—This bonnet of hand-worked eyelet on muslin is an example of a bonnet that was both fancy and functional.

FIG. 28.—Bonnet of sheer blue chambray (circa 1860) is lined with rose-colored muslin; it is stiffened with several layers of fabric and stitched vertically across the brim. The bavolet measures 14½ inches.

assumed this characteristic shape, which was soon followed by the poke bonnet that sat farther back on the head, but continued to be tied under the chin with ribbons (Fig. 25). From that time on through the remainder of the century, fancy bonnets became smaller and more elaborately trimmed. Lucadia Pease wrote from Austin in 1855: "What rediculous [sic] bonnets are worn now. Mine is white uncut velvet with a profusion of ribbons and flowers" (Hart and Kemp, 1974). Another lady boasted about doing her own "millinary" using a purchased bonnet frame and $2 worth of blonde lace and flowers. One good black bonnet of velvet and satin or silk with lace, ribbons, even streamers down the back, as the one shown in Fig. 26, was a part of every lady's wardrobe. Handled gingerly, stored away in special boxes or baskets when not in use, and retrimmed occasionally, that good bonnet could be worn for a decade or more for "Sunday best."

Owning a fancy bonnet was important, but owning a sunbonnet was a necessity. Some were both fancy and functional (Fig. 27). Designed for outdoor wear, the sunbonnet boasted a ridged brim, often with a ruffle around the front and sides and a capelike portion, called a bavolet or curtain, to protect the neck. The stiffened brim was achieved with several layers of fabric, one of which was customarily of crinoline, stitched in a myriad of quilted lines and designs. There were quiltings of diamonds varying from ¼ to 1¼ inches

FIG. 29.—Blue chambray dress (1908-1910) has eyelet trim; the wide-brimmed white muslin bonnet is lined with blue chambray. Little girl's dress (1880) is made of striped gingham.

FIG. 30.—Black hickory split bonnet (removable stays in brim are made of split hickory) is made of sturdy cotton twill and trimmed with hemmed double ruffles. It was originally worn in Kentucky and dates from 1880.

FIG. 31.—This gingham slat sunbonnet is made up in navy shadow pane check on white with pink chambray brim lining and rick-rack edging. It is typical of the slat bonnet favored for the last quarter of the 19th century.

in size. Some were stitched in squares, curves, lozenges, or hexagons—the design spontaneously created by the seamstress, as shown in Figs. 28 and 29.

Goods used to fashion sunbonnets were as diverse as the women who wore them. Calico, coarse muslin (both solid and printed), checkered gingham, chambray, sateen, fine sheer wool crepe, wool rep, silk taffeta, and even curtain scrim were some of the choices. The important role of the black mourning bonnet is reflected in the large number that have survived the years. They are made in the same variety of fashion as the more colorful sunbonnets and are found in sateen, wool brilliantine, silk taffeta, muslin, velvet, padded china silk, as well as black calico (Fig. 30).

About mid-century, the slat bonnet appeared (Figs. 30, 31). In bonnets of this type, horizontal lines were stitched as casings in the six to eight inch brim, and thin slats of hickory or cardboard were inserted for stiffening. Many of the bonnets are cleverly cut so that they flatten for ironing and have drawstrings to puff and shape them. Trims vary from eyelet to rickrack, self-ruffle to lace, or a combination of different trims. Many bonnets were left plain with no attempt to fancy them up.

An occasional bonnet appears with the lining of the brim made of a contrasting color. The blue chambray with an exaggerated long curtain shown in Fig. 28 has a self-ruffle and a rose-colored lining in the brim. The fine white eyelet-trimmed bonnet in Fig. 29 boasts an exceptionally wide brim, lined with pale blue chambray.

Eventually, published instructions could be found in periodicals to guide the seamstress in the making of a "Ladies' Sun-bonnet." One was sketched and described in an 1891 *Delineator* as being "disposed in a series of soft folds, which are graduated large toward the top, where they stand quite high, with picturesque effect." There was a curtain buttoned to the crown and intended to "fall with pretty fullness over the shoulders." This style of bonnet required 2⅜ yards of 27 inch material. The bavolet (or neck ruffle) might vary in length from 2½ inches to 14½ inches.

By the middle 1890s sunbonnets could be ordered by mail. Montgomery Ward & Co. offered them for little girls as well as for women. One with a "peek-a-boo front" and Normandy back (an English style of shaping the crown) made of white pique or "washing gingham" could be had for fifteen or twenty cents, depending on the age of the child. Women's models cost a few cents more. Black and white checked percale bonnets of large, medium, or small check with lace edging on the two fluted ruffles were twenty-five cents.

Photographs from The Museum Collection are convincing proof of the importance of bonnets. Little girls wore miniature models of those of their mothers' (Fig. 29). Even infants were properly bonneted. On the prairie frontier the sunbonnet became a signature acceptable for wearing in all sorts of situations. It could appear very businesslike when worn for utilitarian purposes, but it often had a coquettish appeal and provided little protection, other than to hold the hair in place, when donned by a young girl ready for an outing.

The Apron—Useful and Ornamental

The apron was such an important part of a lady's wardrobe that in the late 1700s it came out of the kitchen and was considered proper "even in full dress." For years two types continued to appear—the useful and the ornamental.

White aprons seem to have been favored throughout most of the nineteenth century, and they were worn almost as consistently by the lady on the frontier as were sunbonnets. Nationwide, even on the wagon trains and the new frontiers, women clung to starched white aprons and petticoats, along with a touch of ribbon, as if to denote their role, in spite of activities that seemed to challenge it. For the most part, the thrifty pioneer ladies fashioned their aprons out of any type fabric that was at hand—homespun, linen, cotton, or even bleached feed sacks. Sometimes a dress length would allow enough material to make a matching apron. But a white apron was always worn "for good."

Sheer aprons, popular for years, often appeared as tea aprons. Black china silk embroidered with scarlet or purple feather-stitching held favor. This type

FIG. 32.—A striped calico bibbed apron (1870) is shown here over a gray calico one-piece day dress. The bonnet is made of heavy white muslin with a pale pink lining and hand-crocheted edging.

was copied in heavier black fabric for more utilitarian purposes. Most aprons were long enough to reach the lower skirt edge. Sometimes the corners were rounded off to give an attractive shaping to an otherwise plain length of goods. Trims of crocheted lace or embroidered flounce from an old petticoat made decorative additions to a white apron. A plain, printed apron was often dressed up with a "frill of its own stuff," a self-ruffle.

Aprons were not neglected in the fashion periodicals. In 1870 *Harper's Bazar* gave instructions for making a muslin kitchen apron with a bodice like the one shown in Fig. 32. The measure of this apron was 37 inches long and 73 inches around the lower edge. Another apron of the 1870s was made of coarse linen with cross-stitch design in red and blue, intended to be a tea apron. Cross-stitch worked on checked gingham was another popular version. Many aprons were simply shaped pieces of calico with suspender straps, very plainly finished with machine-stitched edges.

On the Texas frontier, when almost any occasion could be turned into a form of entertainment, young folks often had a "calico apron party." The men were given a partially completed calico apron and challenged with hemming it; girls had a length of calico to fashion into a tie. When the work was done, the couples were paired off by matching the material of apron and tie. It was a great game of chance and suspense. The man with the best job of hemming was rewarded with a fancy cake.

Soon after the turn of the century, the young periodical *Peoples Popular Monthly* offered an inducement in an effort to win subscribers: "Apron Pattern Given." New subscribers could have a full year subscription and real apron pattern for twenty-five cents. "This is a Prize Pattern offered in 3 sizes," they claimed. How many of the aprons that appeared on the frontier were made up by a pattern would be difficult to surmise, but a variety of styles are shown throughout this publication, thus recording the popularity of aprons and the resourcefulness of the women who fashioned them. Based on the ingenuity and enterprising practices of the women, it is safe to assume that few were made from a pattern.

At Home Wear—The Wrapper

Carrying the distinction of frontier dress almost as marked as the bonnet and apron was the wrapper. It was a garment repeatedly in evidence, with written and pictorial records of its popularity. Mention was made as early as 1830 in a newcomer's letter of "neighbor ladies dressed in neat wrappers" who came to call (Pennybacker, 1888).

The wrapper appeared throughout the remainder of the century, changing little in form. Its appeal, first and foremost, lay in its comfort. Early Butterick catalogues offered a mid-Victorian version of the wrapper under the guise of "comfortable negligee." The wrapper followed much the same style; less fitted than dresses, it required no bustles, hoops or corsets, was relatively easy to make, and was practical for the active woman. Not to be ignored, too, was its adaptability for maternity wear.

FIG. 33.—Wrapper (1880s) of sprigged black calico was worn by a homesteader who moved from Arkansas to the Indian Territory before settling in Callahan County. The slat bonnet is fashioned of white calico.

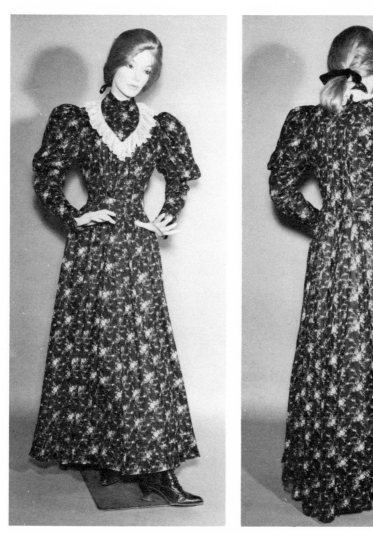

FIG. 34.—This "dressy" wrapper of watered floral print on black boasts the Watteau pleat.

The wrapper was a long cover-up, made with a high neck, long sleeves and full, flowing body. Even though it appears to be an unrestrained fashion, most wrappers were made with an inner bodice or lining attached at the side seams, and buttoned snugly over the bust. Fullness in the back of the wrapper was contrived, front and back, through a series of gathers, pleats, or shaped panels. Extra fullness was concentrated in the center back, oftentimes in the so-called "Watteau" pleat—a grouping of box pleats from the neck to the waistline, hanging loosely from the shoulders. The Watteau look, which was referred to "variously" in fashion descriptions of the nineteenth century, was derived from a fashion inspired by the eighteenth-century French artist Antoine Watteau.

FIG. 35.—Tan and white plaid gingham was used to fashion this "Mother Hubbard" (1880s) with Watteau pleats and ruffled bertha. White sunbonnet has Valenciennes lace edging.

The fashions he painted were distinguished by gowns that fell directly from the shoulders at the back into voluminous folds. Both wrapper and tea gown featured the graceful Watteau look. Even the most ordinary homemade calico wrapper followed this trend (Fig. 33).

Variations in construction can be found in wrappers that are semi-fitted in front and loose in the back; there are those that have just a lining in the yoke, and a few that are fully lined. A very special wrapper documented in The Museum Collection is one of black cotton, printed in a watered floral design of rose, green, and light yellow (Fig. 34). It has the Watteau pleat, caught in at the waistline. The lining is of four different types of fabric—gray floral

FIG. 36.—Wrappers of sheer cotton were favorites at the turn of the century and were popular choices for neighborly socials. The black silk apron was important for special occasions.

FIG. 37.—Choice of fabric and accessories made this black wool wrapper serve as "Sunday best" for many years for a lady near Colorado City. The black velvet bonnet fits closely around the head, with a high, full crown.

print, tan checked gingham, coarse tan muslin, and firm gunmetal sateen. Buttons and buttonholes adorn both the lining and the wrapper. Not only is it unusual for the wrapper to be fully lined, it also is unusual for both lining and wrapper to fasten visibly.

The wrapper chosen by the lady on the frontier was made of many different fabrics: calico, printed percale, gingham plaid, dotted lawn, and wool challis. The season determined to a large degree the fabric choice. Toward the end of the nineteenth century, even though calico had become very inexpensive by the yard, wrappers could be ordered ready-made at such a low price that many women secured them through mail order for as little or less than it would cost to make one. They were available for morning or mourning, for house gowns, and for tea gowns. Elaborate versions of the wrapper were dubbed hostess gowns and appeared in silk, cashmere, alpaca, and bengaline, trimmed with watered silk chiffon, black lace, or elegant braid and ribbon. These were popular choices for entertaining or receiving at home, particularly in urban communities and military outposts.

The Hubbard, or "Mother Hubbard," as the wrapper was sometimes called, was worn loose or belted. Why it was called a "Mother Hubbard" is unclear, unless it referred to the nursery rhyme. The plaid gingham of the 1880s shown in Fig. 35 has the standard muslin fitted inner-bodice, as well as fitted, muslin undersleeves, and a matching crushed belt. This type wrapper required 10 yards of 28-inch wide material for construction. Only a few examples with separate belts have been found. A sheer wrapper of printed lawn with a demi-belt in back and half belts that cross in the front is pictured in Fig. 36.

In the early 1890s a wrapper of dark print, much like that in Fig. 33, with lined waist and ruffles over the shoulders could be ordered for fifty-nine cents. The one illustrated was made by the lady who wore it. Its length indicates that she was just under 5 feet tall with a waist measurement of 23 inches, judging by the lining, which was shaped from much-laundered feed sacks that still retain some of the printing. Because of her small size, indicating the need for less material, and her frugal practices, this little lady probably managed to make her wrapper for less than one could be ordered ready-made. Turkey red calico was available by mail order from the Sears, Roebuck and Co. catalogue for five cents per yard.

When women ordered by mail from Montgomery Ward & Co. in 1895, the bust size was the only measurement required for a summer wrapper of new light print that could be had for as little as 59 cents or as much as $1.75. A ladies' tea gown made in the same fashion of finest all wool French "challie" with Watteau pleats and wide cape sleeves of China silk was priced at $9. A more tailored version of the wrapper in Henrietta cloth (a fine twilled silk and wool fabric, which could be furnished in all seasonable shades) was also $9. This choice might become the "Sunday Best" for some women, as shown in Fig. 37.

Easily available, varied in fabric offerings, utilitarian, and easy to wear, the wrapper enjoyed widespread popularity (Figs. 38, 39). Even little girls dressed

FIG. 38.—The wrapper, as well as the shirtwaist and skirt, was popular for "at home wear" in early 1900s. (Photograph from collection of The Museum, Texas Tech University.)

in "hubbards," although theirs were sometimes made from daddy's old calico shirt or the skirt of mother's discarded dress.

SKIRT AND SHIRTWAIST

Developing, along with the wearing of the wrapper for everyday, was the practice of combining a separate bodice or waist with a skirt. While this mode first applied to silks and fancy fabrics in the mid 1800s, the practical idea of letting a skirt do double duty soon caught on with women everywhere. A bodice could be made for a fraction of the cost and labor of constructing a full dress. It simplified the cleaning problem and offered variety to a lady's wardrobe. The two-piece approach carried over into everyday wear and answered a need for the busy pioneers. The separate waist or bodice appeared in matching material, in a contrasting solid or print, or in white. By the 1890s, when the true shirtwaists were introduced, they became a favorite fashion for women in all walks of life and in all geographic areas.

A wide choice was noted among the waists discussed in *Godey's Lady's Book and Magazine* of 1864:

> They are made up in every imaginable style, some very costly and elaborate, others quite plain. . . .Braiding, chain-stitching, puffs, tucks, fancy buttons, Valenciennes lace and insertion are all extensively used as trimmings.

Two waists to every dress was considered good planning, inasmuch as the waist would wear out before the skirt. It was quite logical that an extra waist could produce the effect of two dresses because "the waist is more noticed."

FIG. 39.—Sometimes the wrapper was for "dressing up." (Photograph from collection of The Museum, Texas Tech University.)

("Waists" had long been the part of woman's dress that covered the body from the shoulders to the waistline. It is also known as a bodice.)

Skirts for everyday wear were, for the most part, long, plain, and full. Basically, they consisted of 6 to 8 yards of material simply "fulled" (a term referring to gathering) onto the waistband. For several decades skirts increased in circumference. In the 1840s they were 126 inches around; in the 1850s they were 170 inches; and by the 1860s they measured over 190 inches. Fashionable frocks were 7 to 8 yards or over 250 inches around. Fullness might be gauged, gathered, or pleated. Most of the skirts were unlined, and, even if sewn by hand, did not require a great deal of time to make. The one illustrated earlier in Fig. 21 is five lengths of 24-inch printed brown calico. Its style and color, with a slight variation in the printed design, is identical to another skirt worn by the same woman who brought them from the Indian Territory to De Leon, Texas. Both of the skirts originally had matching, separate waists. There is a matching apron for one; for the other there is a matching waist. It was customary to team a skirt with a white bodice or waist and a fancy, trimmed white apron for a dressier touch. Striped cotton, dark print, homespun, novelty cord, plaid gingham, and solid percale were some of the skirt fabrics chosen by the pioneer ladies.

So basic was the style of the long, full, separate skirt, it is difficult to date them. For a long time the skirt fullness was evenly distributed onto the waistband, and although fashion decreed the movement of most of the fullness to the rear by the late 1860s, the simple gathered look continued to be used for many years. These skirts were always worn over many petticoats.

Gradually the skirt lengths began to take on some shaping so that there was less fabric at the waistline. When the gathering is concentrated on the sides and back, with the length extending to the floor, it is safe to assume the skirt dates in the last quarter of the century. The maize calico shown in Fig. 40 has a skirt constructed in this manner. The basque (a fitted bodice that extends over the waist) matches the skirt, retaining the look of a one-piece garment.

Throughout the remainder of the century, even the everyday waists are found made up of diverse fabrics—some very plain, others elaborately trimmed (Figs. 41, 42). The frontier choices include calico, striped and patterned sturdy cotton, muslin, corded ottoman, checked gingham, white of varied weights and qualities, printed lawn in delicate colors, as well as deep pink and blue chambray.

More waists than skirts have stood the test of time, substantiating the fact that the skirt had either worn out or served double-duty by offering length that could be recycled as an apron or a little girl's dress or a little boy's shirt. In some cases, no doubt, the skirt was worn until the brightness was gone and was then discarded.

The term waist took a positive definition in the 1880s, becoming known as the shirtwaist. Although it did not assume the form of buttoning up the front to a convertible collar, it opened in a variety of ways: center front, center

Fig. 40.—Skirts and waists often were constructed of matching fabrics, as in this maize calico (1880s). The bonnet is of blue checked gingham and is made from one piece of fabric; the brim buttons to the crown to provide shaping.

FIG. 41.—This black printed calico skirt (1890s) is shown with Swiss embroidered muslin shirtwaist.

Fig. 42.—A black wool albatross skirt (1890s) is worn with shirtwaist of novelty corded cotton with wide lace bertha and front ruffle. The sunbonnet is of ruffled black wool.

FIG. 43.—The popularity of the "Gibson girl" blouse is evident here. (Photograph from collection of The Museum, Texas Tech University.)

back, sometimes at the side front, but finished at the neck with a high-standing collar (often boned with stays to maintain its upright look). The sleeves were a fascination of variety.

Charles Dana Gibson, the artist who set the model for the All-American beauty, the Gibson Girl, in his drawings, did much to promote the popularity of the shirtwaist with mannish tailored collars and pleats over the shoulders. Manufacturers and dressmakers capitalized on its appeal with ready-made models, and women followed the trend when they purchased or made their own shirtwaists (Fig. 43).

Not only are there many written references to the shirtwaist in catalogues and manuscripts, there also are countless examples remaining, as well as much photographic evidence, in testimony of its popularity (Figs. 44, 45). It ranged from mannish, tailored versions to dainty versions with lace inserts, hand-embroidery and other fancy trims of ribbons, braid, tabs, and buttons. Frontier trunks reveal fabric choices of gingham, striped percale, lace, silk, fine lawn, mull, coarse muslin, and black sateen—dozens of different types trimmed in a variety of ways. Women wrote about their starched waists, prettily embroidered and lace-trimmed, worn over a fancy camisole; mother's white shirtwaist with lace and high collar with stays in it. Amanda Jackson Hoffman wrote in her diary of a "pretty white organdy waist with shoulder puffs made over pale blue."

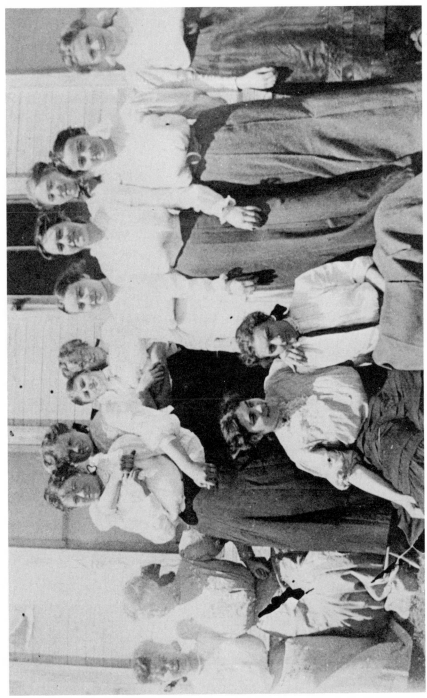

FIG. 44.—The shirtwaist and skirt was favored almost to the point of being a uniform, as shown in this photograph of women at Clarendon College, 1904-1907.

FIG. 45.—The white shirtwaist and dark skirt was a favorite for all sorts of informal wear. This photograph was made on North Spade Ranch in the early 1900s. (Photograph from collection of The Museum, Texas Tech University.)

Skirts at this time were no longer just straight lengths of goods. They were shaped more at the waistline, with fullness concentrated in the center back. The shaping was accomplished with gores that flared toward the ankles where they were often trimmed with flounces and ruffles (Fig. 42). Although the skirt, like the shirtwaist, appears in a variety of fabrics, dark cottons or linen were favored choices, with white and beige linen and pique as summer favorites.

Because the shirtwaist and skirt sizes were easier to standardize, they appear to be among the earliest women's garments to be successfully acquired through mail order. In 1895 printed cotton waists of black and white shepherd check material could be ordered for fifty cents. A Henrietta sateen shirtwaist cost ninety-five cents and one of colored Habutai Japanese silk was $3.75. Inasmuch as a skirt cost only thirty cents if made of gray poplin or $1.25 of black sateen, a woman could make a pretty decent appearance for very little expense. By the turn of the century the availability of these two garments was

FIG. 46.—This sheer batiste shirtwaist has lace yoke and tuckings. The black skirt is lined, interlined, and edged with black velvet binding, and is looped up at hemline (1890).

so great that they could sometimes be found in the general stores. Still, the average woman preferred to make her own, sometimes devoting months to the intricate embroidery and insertions and laces of her shirtwaist (Fig. 46).

FROM POINT OF THE NEEDLE TO ORDERED BY MAIL

THE NEEDLE AS A TOOL

Because the welfare of a family depended to a large degree on someone's skill with the needle, all women were expected to know how "to sew plain." It was a requirement in the art of housewifery and was accomplished with the most basic of tools: an iron, a pair of scissors, and a needle (Fig. 47).

The iron has long been an important sewing tool. It is used to smooth seams, steam and shape curves, produce pleats, and in many ways facilitate the sewing process. Some irons had openings for insertion of hot coals, charcoal, bricks, or heated metal slugs; others were fashioned of cast iron. The earliest flat or sadiron, "sad" meaning "heavy," was hand-wrought with the handle attached. It eventually appeared with a detachable handle, and weighed from one to nine pounds. There were double-pointed irons, tailor's irons, and those for specific purposes, such as sleeve irons, polishing irons, and fluting irons. The fluting irons had corrugated parts that were heated for making "ruffles with ridges" (Lantz, 1970). In 1866 *Godey's Lady's Book* made this announcement:

> We are at last able to recommend a reliable fluting machine. It consists of two corrugated wheels turned by a crank and heated by means of a lamp placed underneath. The material runs between these wheels and passes out in perfect flutes. [Kerr, 1951]

Scissors were a necessary tool, sold at one point with other sewing implements at the "Toy Shoppe" (akin to a modern gift shop). They were of two types: those with spring action, now known as shears, and those with pivoted blades. Although their style has changed little from ancient Roman times, improved precision crafting techniques changed the materials from which they were made. By the seventeenth century there were skilled scissorsmiths, especially in France. For centuries the scissors have been valued highly by homemaker or tailor (Groves, 1983).

The equally cherished needle has always been an important tool in history. Although it has been fashioned from various materials, it was usually made of metal, which required specialized craftsmen to scour, point, and "hole" it by hand. Because it was not always plentiful, the needle was carefully preserved and carried in a needle case, sometimes clustered with other sewing tools attached to the waist. Eventually these items were suspended by chains from a decorative clasp and worn as an accessory fastened to the belt. This appendage was called a chatelaine (Fig. 48).

In mid-nineteenth century this earlier fashion of wearing the sewing implements attached to the belt was revived, and women wore fanciful tools like the "pretty, quaint chatelaine, once the delight of our great-grandmothers." Although of relatively inexpensive materials, the chatelaine could be extremely decorative. The large clasp that slipped over the waist belt was as important as the tools themselves (Groves, 1973). These became more and more elaborate until the late 1800s, when they went out of style.

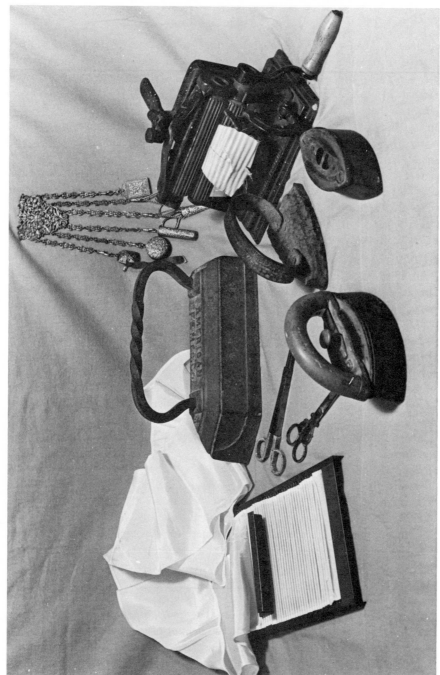

FIG. 47.—Sewing aids: pleater, scissors, goffering iron, tailor's iron, chatelaine, fluting iron, "spare" sad iron, homemade iron, and sad iron.

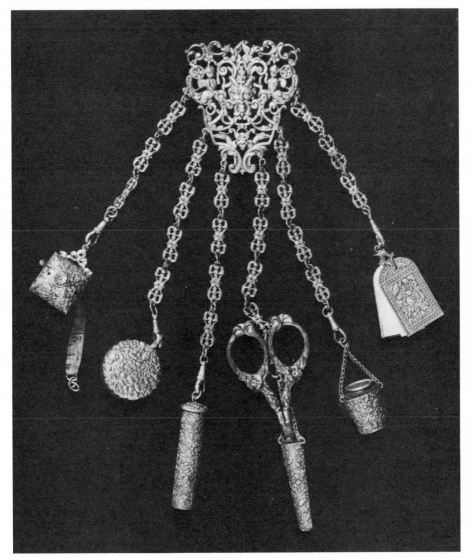

FIG. 48.—A decorative accessory, the English chatelaine, with ivory memory aid, thimble holder, scissors, needle case, pin cushion, and silk tape, was worn attached to the belt.

DEFT FINGERS, SERENE MIND

Encouragement in the use of the needle, as well as practical advice, was bountiful in the nineteenth century. Books, periodicals, and even newspapers played up its importance. A proper task for a lady was to develop the ability to sew a fine seam. A commentary on the importance of the needle to a lady appeared in *The Ladies Hand-book of Plain Needlework* in 1842:

> No one can look upon the Needle without emotion; it is a constant companion throughout the pilgrimage of life. We find it the first instrument of use placed in the hand of the budding childhood, and it is found to retain its usefullness and charm even when trembling in the grasp of fast declining age. [Arnold, 1972]

The needle, so miniature of size and yet of such magnitude in importance, was the tool that made it possible for a woman to clothe the family and create objects that expressed her love of beauty. She was encouraged from all directions to exercise her prowess:

> Nothing will aid you so much in the practice of economy in your dress as expertness with your needle. No American woman, let her speak all the tongues, and play on all the instruments invented, can be said to be educated, if she is not a good needlewoman. With a little pains, you may learn to make your own gowns, with ingenuity, you can turn and refit them. [Kerr, 1951]

Thus advised the editor for *Godey's Lady's Book* in December 1852.

Recorded in the archives are accounts relating to the importance of the needle. One lady wrote about the scarcity of domestic prints, needles, and pins, confiding that they often resorted to mesquite thorns for pins. "In appreciation for three needles (Nos. 6, 8, and 10) Mrs. Barr received a fine ham and two pounds of coffee" (Barr, 1913).

The women who settled on the frontier brought with them their skills and their love of and intrinsic need for beauty. Evidence of this is found in the mounds of fine needlework preserved in attics and trunks. This skill signified more than the ability to trim and beautify a garment; it was a mark of upbringing. Young girls began their lessons with the needle very early, just as their mothers had done. Dutifully and laboriously, they practiced an assortment of stitches and recorded them on samplers, and dated and signed them.

> The pen, the plough, the sword to man we leave,
> But ours the needle from the days of Eve

read one nineteenth century sampler. The artist was usually eleven to thirteen years old (Fig. 49). The inclusion of pious verses was very much the vogue; however, it was not always with enthusiasm that this task was tackled, a fact made obvious in the following message embroidered on a sampler by a little girl:

> Patty Polk did this and she hated every stitch she did in it. She loves to read much more! [Davis, 1974]

Nevertheless she dutifully executed the required assignment, in proof that "Here the needle plies its busy task."

Girls were taught to do the following stitches with propriety: over-stitch, hemming, running, felling, back-stitch and run, buttonhole-stitch, chain-stitch, whipping, darning, gathering, and cross-stitch. Usually the teacher was mother or grandmother, but at least one young woman learned from the nuns in the convent in France where she went to school. "She learned to sew with infinitesimal stitches," as did her maid (Pickrell, 1970).

FIG. 49.—All little girls were expected to develop a prowess with the needle, which they accomplished by working a sampler that they signed and dated.

Beautiful embroidery was considered a mark of refinement in taste and useful accomplishment. An 1865 issue of *Godey's*, the most popular ladies' American magazine, carried a long article on the advantages of needlework for ladies, quoting prose poetry of the late "lamented" Nathaniel Hawthorne:

> Methinks it is a token of healthy and gentle characteristics, when women of high thoughts and accomplishments love to sew, especially as they are never more at home with their own hearts than while so occupied . . . . The slender thread of silk or cotton keeps them united with the small, familiar, gentle interest of life.

So widespread was this theory that proficiency with the needle was the aim of most women and girls. Their skills did not end with simple sewing or with embroidering. Many of them made their own lace. Instructions abounded for wave braid lace, point lace, and laces that were crocheted, tatted, or knitted, or made with a bobbin or needle. Guided by detailed professional directions, anyone could create fine trim (Fig. 50). Still in the possession of Texas families are pattern books published before 1840, with instructions for making lace and fancy needlework. Some of these books were brought directly from Germany

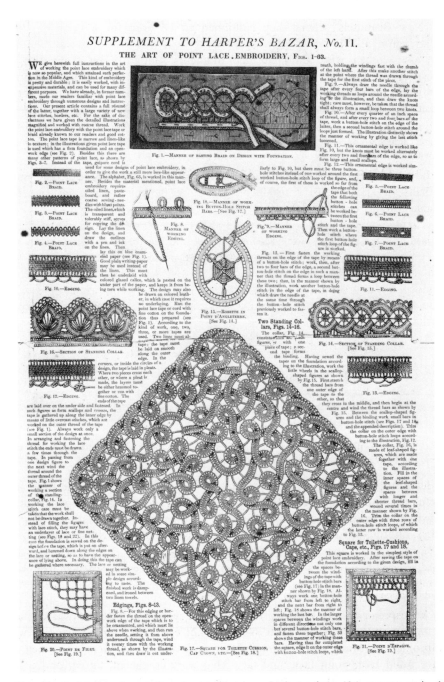

FIG. 50.—Instructions for needlework abounded in periodicals of the 19th century, as in this *Harper's Bazar* supplement of 1874. Point lace was used to trim dresses, to make collars, even to fashion full cloaks and wraps.

to New Braunfels, where they continued to be used for a very long time (Carrington, 1975).

Most women who knew no idle moments knitted when they were not engaged in housework or caring for the children. They knitted laces for petticoats, sheets, even trims for the window shades and bequeathed the legacy of needlework to their children.

> She insisted that her daughters and granddaughters knit. In order to encourage them to knit, Sophie would unwind the thread and insert a cookie, ribbon, small book, sox, or a note. When the child knitted thus far, she got a reward. [Carrington, 1975]

It was the general belief that deft fingers helped produce a serene mind. Results of such industry produced the store of fine needlework found in underpinnings, laces, and embroideries that have survived to this day. An excellent example is shown earlier in the detail of whitework of the muslin pelerine in Fig. 12. So widespread was the addiction to fancy trims that hardly a family exists that hasn't an embroidered petticoat, chemise, nightgown, lace collar, crocheted lace, or length of tatting that was made in the nineteenth century by a great-grandmother or distantly related aunt. Lace and fancy flounces were cherished for generations and used over and over again on various garments.

GIRDED WITH "COMMON SENSE"

Estranged as she was from society and modern developments, the lady on the frontier engaged in the time-consuming task of stitching by hand her garments and those of her family. Then came an invention that was to revolutionize woman's world: the sewing machine. It was considered by some as one of the most important inventions of the nineteenth-century America and was probably as awe-inspiring to many nineteenth-century people as a space capsule was to their twentieth-century descendents.

Although the efforts of many went into the attempts to produce a sewing machine, Elias Howe is credited with patenting the first successful sewing machine in 1846. It was Isaac Singer who improved on and successfully marketed it soon after (Kidwell and Christman, 1974). Public acceptance was slow and the machine was not mass-produced until 1855. Before long, however, it became the first widely advertised consumer appliance. Newspapers and periodicals began to print advertisements for this revolutionary time-saver, and occasionally a machine appeared in the outlying regions of Texas as early as the 1850s (Fig. 51). Few families were able to acquire one until after the war between the states.

Reminiscences of Sallie Reynolds, a young girl growing up in a settlement near Fort Griffin, chronicled the appearance of the first sewing machine, identified as a "Common Sense" machine, about 1870. Clamped to the table for operation, the machine produced a remarkable chain-stitch. Women came from miles around to witness and experiment with this miracle. Admittedly, the sewing machine sewed very nicely, "nicer than the tailor could do." The

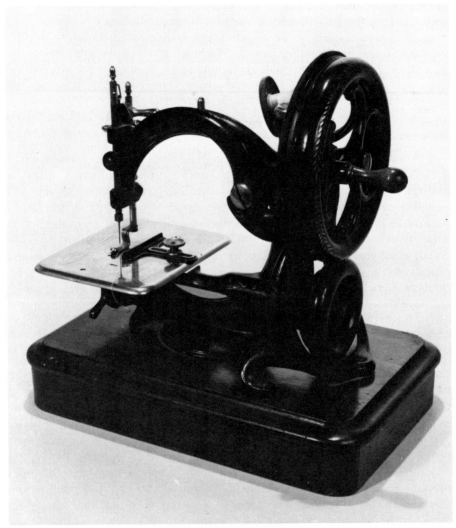

FIG. 51.—Shown here is an early Willcox & Gibbs hand-operated sewing machine. It works on the revolving hook principle, making a chainstitch. Earliest patent date on this machine is 1857; the latest 1871.

wonder of it caused the *New York Tribune* to proclaim by the end of the 1850s: "The needle will soon be consigned to oblivion, like the wheel, and the loom, and the knitting needles" (Kidwell, 1979). This new contraption was soon lauded in periodicals. A testimonial in an 1870 issue of *Godey's* read:

> I have used my Wheeler and Wilson Sewing Machine over ten years without repairs and without breaking a needle, although I commenced use of it without any instructions; have used it constantly for family sewing; have quilted whole quilts of the largest size, and it is still in complete order, runs like a top, and bids fair to be willed to those who come after me with better powers of production than an unbroken prairie farm. Mrs. H.E.G. Arey.

Sewing became less of a time-consuming chore, and the machine offered not only speed but the possibility for greater variety in production.

Sewing machines came in an assortment of brands with bold claims. In 1866 the "celebrated Family Gem Sewing Machine" received the approval of the *New York Tribune*—"with single or double stitch, it silently yet very rapidly does the stitching exactly like hand-sewing." Its cost—$5, including safe delivery (Advertisement *Harper's Weekly* 1866). The "Fairy Gem" was said to be diminutive, fairy-like in size, and was advertised as a "Holiday gift for the work-table." The "Light Running Domestic" claimed to be ever faithful— "Always Ready, Always Willing. Will Last a Lifetime." The new Singer Automatic in 1888 made the claim, "It runs like a breath." There also was the New Singer Vibrator and the New Singer Oscillator.

Production of machines increased annually. Still, the majority of women continued to sew by hand. Even with the major construction by machine, there remained quantities of finishing details that required the use of the needle, in spite of the prediction that the needle would become obsolete.

No Shortage of Fashion News

Of course, there was no standard authority for women's fashions early in the nineteenth century in Texas. There was, in fact, so little opportunity to observe changes that a visitor from the East or a traveler passing through created a stir of excitement with women clamoring for a look at what was new in fashion.

Letters (their writing as well as receiving) were an important therapy to the pioneer woman and offered another means of keeping up with fashion news. In the very early days a woman attired in a dress made by a city dressmaker was considered to be worthy of mention in a letter to friends or relatives back East. Infrequent trips to the nearest supply source sometimes provided a look at the "current mode," because there were some women in the San Antonio, Houston, and Brazoria areas who had fine clothes they had brought with them or ordered from New Orleans. A degree of ambivalence about saving back "good things" is well reflected in a confession made by Mrs. Lucadia Pease in a letter of 1850:

> I fancied from the backwoods look of the place, and the small plain looking houses that I might pack up my Sunday best fixins, to emerge again only when I left here. . . . When our first visitors came, made no change in my dress to see them, thinking fashion could not have reached this remote corner—and was much surprised to see my visitors in silks, with laces and under sleeves which looked fresh from Stewarts. [Hart and Kemp, 1974]

A few years later Mrs. Pease remarked in another letter that Texas ladies ". . . all wear very rich dresses at balls and making calls. . . . It strikes northerners so oddly to see ladies issuing from log houses, arrayed in such an amount of fine and costly dress." Then she continued on to describe the attire of one of her callers in 1854:

> The dress was of cherry colored tissue, embroidered with bunches of flowers in every shade
> of color of the rainbow—it was made with flowing sleeves and the remainder of the arm
> covered with bracelets—nicely fitting blue kid gloves formed a fine contrast to the dress—
> a richly embroidered white lace mantilla was worn far down on the shoulders, a small straw
> bonnet with ribbon and straw colored string. [Hart and Kemp, 1974]

Sometimes a new sleeve style or skirt pattern was requested so that a winter dress could be remade. One woman commented in a letter that she had noticed "some silk dresses with two puffs in front, or rather one on each side," and she pleaded with her sister to try to get a pattern for that new fancy.

By the second quarter of the nineteenth century, fashions were changing more rapidly than at any previous period of history. The world was getting more complex and, along with it, the styles also were more complicated. Several periodicals were initiated and made available for distribution to keep the women informed of these rapidly changing styles. *Graham's American Monthly Magazine of Literature, Art and Fashion* (at one time edited by Edgar Allen Poe) was started in 1826 and appears to be one of the earliest widely distributed American magazines to contain fashion plates (illustrations representing prevailing fashions in wearing apparel).

The first really successful woman's magazine in America was introduced in 1830. *The Lady's Book*, a name later changed to *Godey's Lady's Book and Magazine*, enjoyed immediate and immense popularity and was soon followed by a competitor, *Peterson's Magazine*, in 1841 (Fig. 52). Storehouses of practical advice and entertainments, the periodicals published fiction, articles on etiquette, physical culture, child hygiene, hints on home furnishings, instructions for needlework, and fashion features. Hand-colored fashion plates copied from European illustrations provided women with glimpses of the current fashions. By the 1850s small diagrams of pattern pieces and guides for cutting patterns were included.

Subscribers paid the postage on receipt of the magazines that became available to women in far outposts, and they were circulated through a system of borrowing back and forth between neighbors. The impact of these magazines on frontier families is well illustrated by the following testimony from an 1887 issue of *Peterson's Magazine*:

> There has been a terrible drought in this part of Texas—no rain to amount to anything
> since May, 1885—consequently there are hundreds of families being fed by the relief-
> committee. We had to do without everything we could; but we cannot do without "Petersons,"
> so we sold enough eggs to take it.

Throughout the last decades of the 1800s an increasing number of magazines were being circulated. *Harper's Bazar*, which first appeared in 1867, was called "A Repository of Fashion, Pleasure, and Instruction." It was a weekly publication, selling for ten cents a copy or $4 a year in advance, and "combining the useful with the beautiful, intended for ladies but including things for the full family circle" was the newspaper's claim.

There also was *The Metropolitan*, later to become known as *The Delineator*, *Mme. Demorest's Quarterly Mirror of Fashion*, *McCall's*, *The New York*

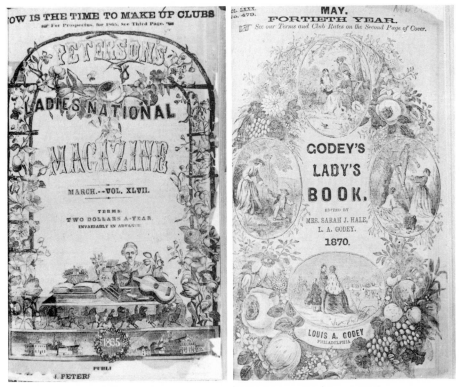

FIG. 52.—Covers of *Peterson's Magazine* and *Godey's Lady's Books.*

Fashion Bazar, The Ladies' Repository, and eventually *The Ladies World* (Fig. 53). A surprising number of folks on the frontier subscribed to one or more of these periodicals, along with *The New York Weekly Sun, Harper's Weekly, The San Antonio Express*, and other newspapers. Every word, even the advertising, revealed something of the outside world and brought it closer to the subscribers.

A REVOLUTION WITH PATTERNS

There was little concern about the need of a pattern for cutting out a dress in the early years. Only the leisure class could afford the luxury of having the fashionable fit that was accomplished by a tailor or mantua-maker, a skilled worker authorized by *The Book of Trades* to cut the more complicated garments.

Masses of women managed to shape fabric and stitch it into a garment with little or no guidance other than an existing garment or lining. Fashion was slow to change, but as the nineteenth century progressed, changes in society and in the rise of the middle class, as well as in style of dress, became more rapid. Women's fashions were more complicated in cut and fit. Although the

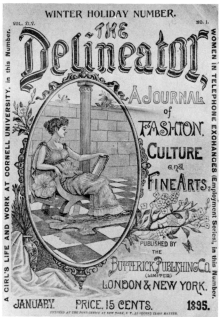

FIG. 53.—Periodicals featuring fashion, culture, and fine arts guided women in the outposts and kept them in touch with the outside world.

old method of accidental fit was no longer satisfactory, patterns for purchase were not available.

Most written advice was found in occasional books, such as *A Treatise on Domestic Economy* published in 1842. One section entitled "To Make a Frock" includes the following instructions:

> The best way for a novice is to get a dress fitted (not sewed) at the best mantua-maker's. Then take out a sleeve, rip it to pieces, and cut a pattern. Then take out half of the waist, (it must have a seam in front). . . . When this is done, a lady of common ingenuity can cut and fit a dress, by these patterns. [Beecher, 1849]

The advice was sound but not practical, inasmuch as most of the mantua-makers were located in the metropolitan areas of the East. They were not only inaccessible, but also were too expensive for consideration by most women on the frontier, so frontier women resorted to their own resources. One Texas lady in Austin in the 1830s described her experience in devising a costume of black and white bombazine:

> . . . for the cutting and stitching and fitting to make sure the blouse shaped properly to the front and fit her well on the shoulders. This, she discovered to be the secret of keeping a blouse from sagging under the arm, the sign of a badly made garment. Being fastidious about the fit of her clothes, she boasted that she thought her venture as a "mantua-maker resulted in a pretty decent appearance!" [Lee, 1962]

This effort was worthwhile, however, to women who thought, according to the morality of the time, that their appearance was an index of character.

Help to the home seamstress came with the advent of *Godey's Lady's Book* and *Peterson's Magazine*, both of which included in their 1850s issues simple diagrams of pattern pieces. The shape was there, but in miniature (Fig. 54). By 1855 *Peterson's* included inch measurements with the diagrams, making the pattern pieces easier to copy. "When *Godey's* began to include inch measurements on its pattern diagrams, the reader was told that the pattern would fit 'a lady of middle height and youthful proportion'" (Kidwell, 1979).

Paper patterns, one size only, soon were offered to subscribers for purchase by the piece or in full. The Editress of *Godey's Lady's Book* listed eight pattern selections in the June 1865 issue that they were prepared to furnish at the prices annexed:

Ladies' Cloaks	$1.25
Ladies' Sleeve	.31
Ladies' Full Dress and Skirt	1.50
Suit for Little Boy	1.00
Dress Body and Sleeve	.30
Children's Cloak	.60
Children's Dresses	.60
Ladies' Under Garments, by the piece	.60

All patterns had to be fitted by a method of pinning to the form, and a lady needed assistance to accomplish this. An 1865 issue of *Godey's* included written instructions for shaping a gored skirt:

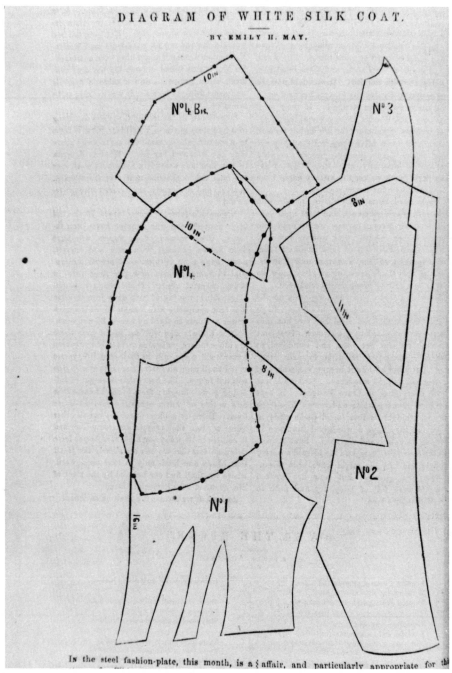

FIG. 54.—Pattern shapes were engraved as fashion plate features in *Peterson's Magazine* of 1865. Guidance left much to the dressmaker's imagination.

Most of the dress skirts are gored, and Mme. Demorest's method of goring is as follows: Fold over six inches on each side of the upper part of the front breadth, graduating this down two-thirds of the skirt, baste this down. The next breadth set one inch below at the bottom, and sew the straight edge to the bias line of the front breadth. Fold a gore of eight inches on the farther side of this breadth, and so continue all around the skirt, setting each breadth one inch below at the lower edge. By this method you have a handsomely gored train skirt without cutting up the material.

Mme. Demorest was considered one of the foremost authorities on fashion. *Mme. Demorest's Quarterly Mirror of Fashion* occasionally included cut tissue pattern pieces in its publication as a bonus.

It was 1863 when Ebenezer Butterick stumbled onto the industry that was to revolutionize women's sewing practices. As his wife cut out a child's dress on the dining room table, she remarked that it would be much easier with a pattern to go by. Mr. Butterick, who had been a tailor, took her suggestion and began to produce patterns for children's clothes and men's shirts that were soon graded in size, notched, and cut of tissue paper. The first Butterick pattern for women was a mid-Victorian version of "at-home wear"—a lady's "wrapper," developed in 1866. A Scotsman, James McCall, founded the McCall's Pattern Company in 1870 in New York. The growth of the pattern business kept pace with the sale of sewing machines, and patterns were soon available from more and more outlets.

The (*Delineator*) Butterick quarterlies, which were the first true counter books, appeared by 1875. Women studied these on the store counter and selected patterns for their home use. If they lived too far away for this service, they could order patterns through various periodicals. *Arthur's Home Magazine* (the monthly recommended by *Godey's* for "those who want a cheaper magazine than the *Lady's Book*") claimed, in an 1874 issue, to be Butterick's Patterns Home Magazine Agency:

As regular agents of E. Butterick & Co., we can now supply, by mail, on receipt of the price, any of their patterns . . . Butterick's patterns are now acknowledged to be the most practical and reliable that are issued, and enable any lady to be not only her own dressmaker, but to appear as well and tastefully dressed as any of her neighbors. See new patterns in this number of *Home Magazine*, with Prices.

Harper's Bazar furnished a pattern supplement that provided shapes and instructions for constructing as many as seventeen different items (Fig. 55). Instructions were sketchy, and the sizing and method of construction were left to the experience and imagination of the seamstress. Each subscriber was expected to trace the pattern, make it up in muslin and alter it before cutting into the precious dress length.

A testimony to the value of this labyrinth of guidance was written by Sallie Reynolds, member of a ranching family near Albany, Texas:

It sounds queer and funny now perhaps but we were going by *Harper's Bazar* and that was a standard authority on all questions of fashion. At that time, the *Bazar* had a fashion sheet with each issue and these patterns had to be traced out by lines of different design, some dotted, some dashed and some of the other kinds. Sister had a tracing wheel with which we would work out these intricate pattern lines. [Matthews, 1958]

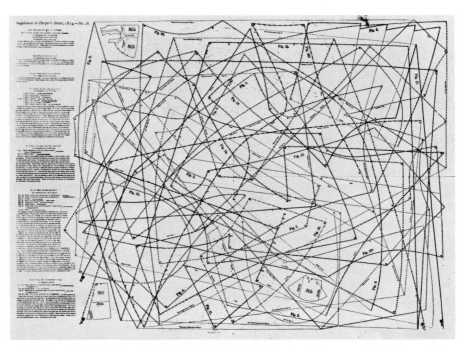

F<small>IG</small>. 55.—In 1870 *Harper's Magazine* included foldout supplements of life-size patterns. Instructions indicated which figures to trace for a complete pattern.

Just such a pattern was used for constructing the wedding dress (Fig. 56) worn by Sallie, a sixteen-year-old bride, in 1876.

Once they acquired a pattern, it was customary to share it with others. Ten yards of muslin was said to be sufficient to cut a pattern. This acquisition was important enough to be recorded in the 1880s in Amanda Jackson Hoffman's diary written in Plainview (Hale County): "Miss Josie cut some patterns for Amanda," who made a beautiful plaid calico dress.

"The great army of women belonging to middle-class circumstances are generally dressmakers for themselves," according to an 1888 issue of *Arthur's Home Magazine*. Although the well-fitting paper patterns and "cheap" pattern books made sewing less of a "bugbear than when lonely women had no guide but a neighbor's dress to assist them," they still challenged the patience and ingenuity of the seamstress. The matter of fitting a pattern properly was not a small one, particularly since a snug, molded look was desired for the basque, and a proper fit was not easily achieved. In 1893 the *World's Fair Premium Tailor System* introduced some improvements for drafting patterns (Fig. 57). The carefully marked pieces of its cardboard patterns were riveted together with slot arrangements to allow movement up and down, in and out, making the pattern easily sized for different measurements. The rigid cardboard was easier to trace than the patterns from *Harper's*. It was not until 1910 that printed instruction sheets were included in a pattern envelope with the pattern

FIG. 56.—*Harper's Bazar* Supplement was used as a guide for making this white alpaca wedding dress for a sixteen-year-old bride in 1876.

FIG. 57.—A cardboard, adjustable pattern with instructions was a part of the *World's Fair Premium Tailor System* patented in 1893.

(Fig. 58). Women all over the Texas frontier eagerly welcomed the opportunities to order patterns, and with so much guidance offered by periodicals, even a timid seamstress could venture into the world of sewing.

KEEPING UP WITH STYLE

The last decades of the nineteenth century reflect more rapid style changes than had been seen in the years of the Texas Republic and early statehood. Even so, greater detailed discussion has been given in this episode of women's fashions to the early years because of the limited examples that exist and sparse materials that are available for investigative study of this period. For the last quarter of the century there was an abundance of periodicals, pattern drafting methods, and commercial patterns. Because there are more

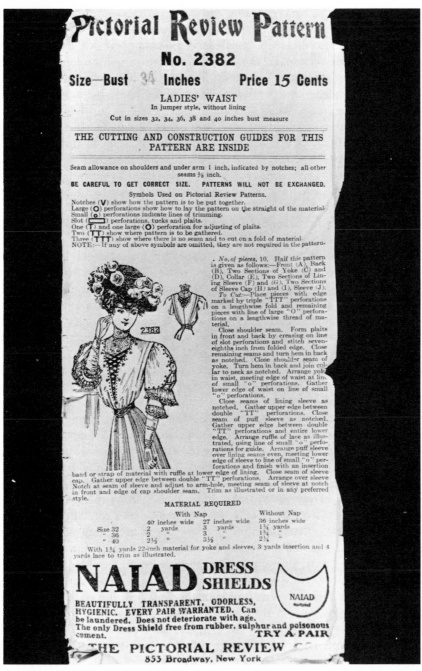

FIG. 58.—By the early 1900s tissue paper patterns appeared with instructions printed on the paper envelope.

printed materials and concrete examples for the student and the historian, the
ensuing style changes will be discussed in more general terms.

While the presence of sewing machines was mentioned in the Houston and
Dallas areas in the 1860s, few families were able to acquire one until after the
War between the States. Throughout the rest of the century the machine
became commonplace, and by 1900 most families, even in outlying districts,
owned one. As the sewing machine was making possible changes in
construction techniques, the dress shape also was undergoing a change.

The succession of changes can be documented in clothes worn by the ladies
on Texas frontiers—whether in the populated coastal regions or on the high
plateau as it was being settled. Women managed to acquire at least an
occasional garment, even if only of calico, that made her feel that she was not
so much out in the backwoods.

As the decade of the seventies set in, skirts continued to be full as they had
been for the preceding forty years. The skirt fullness, however, had moved to
the rear and over it a gathered and looped-up arrangement known as the
polonaise was shaped with the newfangled bustle. The underskirt often boasted
ruffles or pleated flounces. The rather short-waisted bodice, made separate,
was fitted snugly to the figure, buttoning up the front to a small flat collar
or a narrow standing collar band. The shoulder seams continued to be slanted
behind the top of the shoulders. Sleeves were becoming plainer and more fitted
than in the sixties, and the armscye was located at the normal shoulderline
rather than dropping below the shoulder. This up-to-the-minute style is well
reflected in the printed maize calico shown in Fig. 59. A stylized flower pattern
that resembles cotton bolls in rust, brown, and white is scattered on a
vermiculate printed maize background. The long, ruffle-trimmed skirt is
topped with a bodice that extends quite low and is looped back with
complicated draping to form the polonaise. This pattern made up in silk and
fancifully trimmed would take on the look of a party dress or a "best" dress.

Trimmings were often multiple and varied—pleatings, flounces, fringe, braid,
or a combination of several of these. Later in the 1870s there was less fervor
for overtrimming. Two shades of a kindred hue or one color in two different
textures appeared in combination. Colors were interesting—dragon green,
greenish gray, madras, red mahogany, prune (almost black), sphinx gray, and,
on the lighter side, buff, lilac, maize, salmon, pale green, pale blue, and violet.

A slimmer, more vertical and less curved line began to appear in the dresses
of the late 1870s and the early 1880s in the so-called cuirass bodice (a long,
tight bodice descending over the hips) and the princess sheath dress. The bustle
continued to be worn, but it was less exaggerated. Some of these dresses ended
with a pronounced train on the skirt. More commonly, the skirt was floor
length, as seen in the Paisley linen and wool (Fig. 60). The influence of the
princess line was also strongly reflected in the wrapper and teagown discussed
in chapter 3.

This pretty Paisley frock documents the practice of having two fabrics trim
each other. In this case the velvet trims the Paisley and in turn the Paisley

FIG. 59.—This two-piece printed calico polonaise dress (early 1870s) demonstrates well the fact that a pattern could be used for a simple calico as well as for a fancy silk—its degree of elegance depending upon the trim.

trims the velvet. Obviously this dress was valued highly by its owner, because it has evidence of careful needle weaving where the frail areas appear under the arms and around the buttons. As was observed in the earlier classic dress, here again the seamstress resorted to the use of a multiple of different fabrics to make the lining. The concentrated fullness in the back has been held in position by tapes that tie on the underneath from one side seam to the other. This detail of construction is reflected in the naming of this period as the "tied-back time."

By the mid-1880s most of the day dresses, two-piece once again, had a bodice that was longer, sometimes pointing to a deep V in front over the skirt. It continued to be fitted, buttoning up the front to a two-inch wide upstanding collar. Velvet bandings sometimes trimmed bodice front, or the bodice front might be turned back to form revers. Sleeves were plain and narrow. Some dresses retained the draped apron effect; others were decorated with a panel down the front (Fig. 61). About 1885, the bustle was so exaggerated that it became a rigid, shelf-like protrusion with much fullness pleated into the back of the skirt, which swept the floor so that dust ruffles were needed to protect the underskirt, and its lower edge was finished with wool braid or velvet binding. The same pattern could be used for the everyday house dress as well as for the special occasion dress. The difference was in the fabric choice and the elaboration of trim.

Chenille and passementerie, along with ruching, lace, poufs, bretelles, jet beads, and spangles abounded in the 1880s on the fancy clothes. Pleating was used to trim the polonaise and the skirt edge—even the calicoes sometimes. Favorite colors included heliotrope, peacock blue, terra cotta, primrose, brown, cream, fawn, dark blue, and beige, rendered in small delicate patterns, Scotch tweed, stripes, checks and dots. A few of the fabrics available were India silk, cashmere, barred muslin, foulard, albatross, velvet, corded silk, mull, zephyr, and nun's veiling.

As the 1890 decade began, skirts were plainer with the use of scant draperies (Fig. 62). Most of them were made now with shaped gores, fitting snugly over the hips and flaring at the hemline, yet retaining much fullness in the center skirt back. Bustles were very small—just a soft pad. The bodice was fitted closely with shaping and tucks, always lined and structured with metal stays to retain a rigidity of posture. In the early part of the decade, sleeves were only slightly full, set in with a little peak on the shoulder. By 1895 they had expanded to a maximum in the upper part but fitted closely from the elbow to the wrist, easily recognized in the balloon sleeve and the popular leg-of-mutton sleeve, along with modified versions of each.

Because they were easily attainable at a nominal price at this time, the cotton fabrics—muslin, calico, gingham, lawn, and percale—were selected for everyday wear. Calico, no longer in the realm of the unattainable, was held in esteem because it responded so well to laundering and always looked crisp and fresh. It dominated the fabric choices for wrappers as well as for general

FIG. 60.—This fully lined princess sheath (late 1870s, early 1880s) is made of a firmly woven linen-wool combination. The stripes of shades of burnt orange, brown and grayish greens printed on ivory ground are comprised of a popular Paisley design—a variation of the Indian pine cone, on the broad stripes that alternate with a stripe of precisely petaled flowers. Brown velvet is used to trim and accent this striking print.

Fig. 61.—A young lady of sixteen poses in her fashionable two-piece dress (mid 1880s). The bodice, which has now taken the form of a basque, is made separate from the skirt and has a shaped peplum extending over the skirt. (Photograph from collection of The Museum, Texas Tech University.)

wear dresses. While silks were favored for dressy costumes, there were fancy cottons available that were also popular—sateen, printed cotton twill, such as the feather printed blue (Fig. 62), that closely resembles a challis in appearance.

As the century was drawing to a close, almost any color could be found, but among those favored were eminence purple, myrtle green, magenta, Hussar blue, old rose, peach, red and ruby. Black, as it had been for twenty years, was the choice for many ladies. It was always considered smart to have a "good black silk" that could last for several decades. This subject is discussed in a later section and is well illustrated in Fig. 63.

The practice of migrating from one settlement to a new frontier was not uncommon for people who came to Texas. As the railroad reached toward the north and across the state, supplies were easier to acquire in certain areas. This created distinct contrasts in lifestyle of people as near as 100 miles apart. As late as the 1890s the South Plains could be reached only by wagon train; therefore supplies were more limited in this area than elsewhere. These women continued to meet the challenge of how to acquire their costumes or the goods for creating them.

THE DRUMMER AND THE MERCANTILE

Through the years of settlement women faced the question of where to obtain a measure of goods to meet the needs of the family. Drummers, who were commercial travelers, made infrequent rounds with all manner of goods stocked in their wagons or rolled in their packs. A drummer's visit was a thrill to the isolated rural folks, and the family would gather round and give him the place of honor (Clark, 1964).

Mary Moore Prideaux, in an unpublished essay entitled "Early Days on the Llano Estacado," describes the importance of the drummer at Fort Graham. Drummers were frequently immigrants like Constantine Salome, a native of Damascus, who, with his brother Tiras, visited Fort Graham in the 1870s. With a flourish, he would unstrap the leather fastenings on his wagon and roll back the awning to reveal colorful bolts of goods and a rush of smells from sachet, soaps, and leather—a veritable variety store. He had all manner of sewing notions: thimbles, needles, laces, ribbons, trims and toilet articles, even fancy combs. At Fort Graham, Constantine would leave many yards of calico, which he sold at four yards for thirty cents. It was a boon to the ladies who frequently could work out a trade: a chicken or a dozen eggs for a yard of calico, or eggs and butter for needles, stockings, combs, and brushes.

An emissary or "agent" on the supply wagon chose the fabric when supply outlets were too distant for the entire family to make the trip. In time, of course, mercantile stores were established near enough in most areas to allow women to make their own selections. On rare shopping excursions, the barter system again seemed to work effectively. Eggs, cotton seed, and butter packed

FIG. 62.—This leaf-printed one-piece cotton dress, of a quality that resembles wool challis, has black lace trim at the neck, the surplice opening, and the sleeves. It served as a good dress in the 1890s for a ranch woman in Terry County.

FIG. 63.—Black wool dress with tucked tulip skirt and lace-trimmed bodice has fine dressmaking details that mark it with the professional touch.

in a wash tub were exchanged for all sorts of things. Amanda Jackson Hoffman's diary recorded such facts: $135 cents [*sic*] worth of butter got me two dresses, 3 pr. hose and some thread, and Tood enough jeans to make him two pr. pants."

Sutler's stores sprang up in the vicinity of the forts and offered a variety of merchandise that included sewing notions and some fabrics. The women made purchases there occasionally, and a man would bring back lengths of material for his wife and daughters. "John came from the Fort yesterday. Brought me a new dress. . . ," was an important entry in Amanda Jackson Hoffman's diary.

Relatives and friends in more settled areas or back East would mail out packages with yardage for new dresses, sewing notions, or a new bonnet. One young bride suffered disappointment when the goods shipped out from Houston for her wedding dress arrived one month late. The package, sent by express, had been so long enroute that it was worn through and the fabric was frayed.

Anyone who traveled "to the city" would oblige his neighbors by filling requests for special purchases—fancy trims, a skirt length in silk, or a piece of calico. A man would bring dainty articles of wearing apparel from the markets of New Orleans or a "dress pattern," which meant a length of printed goods, enough to make a dress. Occasionally several members of the family would ride into the nearest supply source, Galveston, Colorado City, or Fort Worth, and spend two or three days selecting goods, new hats, shoes, and sewing notions for their wardrobes for the next season.

On her way to the Centennial Exposition in Philadelphia, Sallie Reynolds' sister stopped in Fort Worth to purchase white silk alpaca for Sallie's wedding dress and brought it back to Fort Griffin. The two sisters then made up the wedding dress and the "second day" dress using The Supplement and pictures from *Harper's Bazar* (Figs. 55, 56).

New Orleans was Texas' major source of imported dress goods even during the Civil War. From the 1850s on, however, various types of cloth became increasingly available in stores in Houston, Galveston, Austin, Dallas, and Fort Worth. By the 1880s dealers of dry goods and supplies were plentiful in most major cities. From Houston, a merchant advertised dress goods that he obtained directly from the mills on his semiannual buying trips to New York. He further claimed to import directly much of his foreign stock (The Industrial Advantages of Houston, Texas, and Environs, 1894).

Some men were not convinced that fabric for clothing was a necessity. Women found ways to purchase the goods, although their means might have been devious. Mrs. Mamie Wolffarth Jackson and Mrs. Stella Wolffarth, in a tape entitled "Early Lubbock History," relate the tale of F. M. Burns Dry Goods in Colorado City charging out four barrels of apples to one rancher when, in fact, the merchandise was really bolts of cloth. The head of the house didn't mind paying for food but felt that dress goods were an extravagance.

The Dressmaker

Even in the outposts there were women who did not make their own clothes, particularly those garments for very special wear. Some were able to turn the sewing over to the grandmother, mother, sister, or to make an exchange with a friend, trading another skill for someone's sewing prowess. From the very earliest settlements there were many single ladies and widows who used their skills with the needle as a means of livelihood, inasmuch as dressmaking was a profession they could practice with dignity.

As early as 1840 there were women like Mrs. John Duff Brown, who moved to Austin after she was widowed.

> Her skillful needle became her chief weapon against the wolf that threatened her very door. Before very long, however, she realized that she had established a trade, for in connection with her ability to make the little steel instrument ply in and out, she possessed a certain creative ability, had an eye for design, and what was more to the purpose, could suit the design to the individual wearer. Such ability rarely fails of success. [Pickrell, 1970]

One woman was known to have taken a hatchet in payment for the making of a dress. Mrs. Elizabeth Renny, left with several small children to support in the 1850s, was not appalled with:

> Fine hand-hemmed ruffles for my lady's thing, daintily tucked bosoms for the gentlemen's shirts, dresses elaborate and plain, stretched in some cases over immense hoop-skirts. [Pickrell, 1970]

For the family who could afford it, there was also the professional seamstress who traveled around the countryside armed with a sewing machine. "What an autocrat was the elderly maiden who went from house to house in our childhood, the tailoress or dressmaker of the whole neighborhood, highest authority on both news and fashion" (E. J. Vickers, personal communication). She would take up residence with one family at a time and remain as long as three weeks. One room of the house was devoted to cutting, fitting, and stitching. The machine kept up a steady hum while wardrobes for the next year were turned out for the entire family. Most of these dressmakers earned no more than seventy-five cents a day. The well-organized woman, with a large family to outfit, had the garments cut out before the arrival of the seamstress, having accomplished the cutting by degrees. When the seamstress was gone, every item for personal and household wear was complete. This practice was not uncommon among families affluent enough to hire a seamstress, whose visit usually took place twice a year.

Expert needlewomen, with no particular claim to fame, did dressmaking in their homes. Almost every small town had its Mrs. Rankin or Mrs. Murphy who was the seamstress for a wide region. "So welcome she made us feel, so fascinating her *Delineator*," one young girl wrote about the lady who did her sewing in Central Texas (Spikes and Ellis, 1952).

The height of luxury was to order special things made up by a modiste, a dressmaker who dealt in fashionable dress. Women sent away to Fort Worth, New Orleans, and even as far as Kentucky and South Carolina, where skilled

FIG. 64.—Trousseau or second-day dress of brick red bombazine (1881), trimmed with incised pewter buttons, was especially made by a dressmaker in New York City to be worn in San Antonio.

French ladies did professional sewing. If they had the fabric, it was mailed off with measurements and a description of the desired style. Otherwise, it was necessary to await a shipment of samples from which a selection was made, followed by a long wait for instructions and order to reach the dressmaker. Another interval passed before the finished garment was returned. A special dress was very special (Fig. 64).

Most department stores also were engaged in mail order custom work. Swatches of material and detailed descriptions were provided on request, sometimes including an illustration of the style. Measurements were provided by the customer, who also was requested to send an old lining or waist that fit well.

As communities began to flourish, dressmakers set up establishments, and business was lively. While most dressmakers did not advertise, there were some like Madame Rosemary Jones, "late of Washington, D.C.," who used the press in San Angelo in the 1880s to announce establishment of her dressmaking shop "now operating" (Green, 1974). She promised new ideas and the latest fashions from Paris. Others, like Madame Sanders of Louisville, Kentucky, relied on satisfied customers for advertising and created elaborate gowns for many West Texas ladies. A robin's egg blue silk wedding gown, trimmed with ostrich tips, and a trained coral silk ball gown in The Museum Collection bear labels on the petersham (belt inside the bodice) woven with Madame Sanders' name and the location of her establishment. The elegant brown ciselé velvet and silk with chenille and moire trim shown in Fig. 65 was made to order by Madame Brown of Kansas City, Kansas. While on a cattle drive in Kansas, an Albany, Texas, rancher commissioned the dressmaker to make this walking dress for his wife.

When the railroad branched into their area, some women indulged in the luxury of boarding the train for Fort Worth, Houston, or other metropolitan cities. There they would take a room at the hotel for several days while they were being fitted by the leading modiste for a wardrobe of new frocks (E. J. Vickers, personal communication).

Having something sent from Paris or London was truly a luxury. One young girl remarked that her mother spoke of Paris fashions as if they were almost holy. Envied was the lady who was able to order a bonnet, a cloak, or a length of silk from abroad. Once the steamship was being used extensively in the 1870s, it became a status symbol to sail to Europe for a continental trip that enabled the wealthy rancher's wife to purchase the latest Paris couture fashions while she was there. Other members of the family brought back gossamer sheer embroidered silk from Switzerland, lace shawls from Belgium, and brocades from Italy. The lavish taste that was indulged in during the late nineteenth century is reflected in the elegant items that have been preserved.

Mail Order

Long before most of the homesteaders were living within easy access of a mercantile or emporium, a new world was introduced to them by mail. Advertisers in metropolitan newspapers offered limited goods to be had by mail, sight unseen—a fine imported shawl, a suit for a gentleman, a measure of silk or calico for a lady.

Godey's Lady's Book, widely circulated by 1865, included an advertisement not only for a limited selection of patterns but also a brief list of ready-made items. There were no descriptions or illustrations, but the available merchandise included dresses, double wrappers, cambric skirts, shawls, and children's clothing. The mail order source was not widely used in Texas until later in the century, except by officers' wives in military outposts. They also acquired white silk hose, fine black slippers, and custom-made dresses directly from merchants in Baltimore, New York, and Philadelphia.

"We have no lack of catalogs and fashion plates," commented one officer's wife who received catalogues from Altman's and Doyle and Adolphe's. With mail being delivered three times a week from San Antonio to Fort Concho, catalogues arrived with frequency. Sometimes as many as ten packages at a time were delivered to one lady. This cosmopolitan practice caught on with women whose families had settled near the army posts, and eventually some of the ranchers' wives began cautious ordering.

In 1872 there appeared in the *Montgomery Ward Merchandise Sheet* a one-page listing of "Grangers Supplied by the Cheapest Cash House in America." Among the 163 articles listed were:

12 yards best quality Prints	$1.00
2 Corsetes, Beauty Style, Imported	1.25
2 Lotta Hoop Skirts	1.00
7 yards of Blue Denim	1.00
1 Hoop Skirt, 1 Bustle and 1 Hair Braid	1.00
12 new style Ruches, for the Neck	1.00
16 yard genuine Irish Poplin, all shades, green, light brown, rose, slate and drab	15.00

Within three years this list had become a 3 x 5 inch, 72-page catalogue (Fig. 66), with more than 1,860 items listed. Montgomery Ward & Co., the firm that issued this first catalogue, in time printed the instructions for filling out an order in twelve languages and urged customers to write orders in their native language if they preferred (*1872-1972 A Century of Serving Consumers*, The Story of Montgomery Ward). Certainly this was an enticement for many of the immigrants who were not fluent in the English language.

By 1878 the first fashion illustration to appear in a mail order catalogue was published by Montgomery Ward & Co. (Fig. 67). Since that time, mail order has been a major source for apparel. Because the catalogue was aimed at the general public, the fashion illustrations were never high style and lagged a few years behind fashions available in metropolitan outlets.

Sears, Roebuck and Co. had its beginning in 1866 as the R. W. Sears Watch Company. By 1895 Roebuck had joined the force, and they were producing a 507-page catalogue that offered, in addition to watches and jewelry, women's garments and millinery, wagons, musical instruments, furniture and household goods (Fig. 68).

The mail order catalogue soon became a must for families everywhere; hardly a home anywhere was without one. A short time earlier family necessities were met by infrequent and long wagon trips for supplies. Now most needs of the family could be filled by mail. It was observed in *Merchant*

Fig. 65.—A modiste in Kansas City was commissioned to make this dress of coupe de velvet with satin and chenille for a rancher's wife (1886).

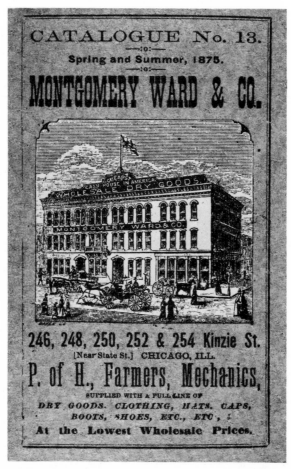

FIG. 66.—Montgomery Ward & Co. catalogue of 1875.

to the Millions, a brief history of the origins and development of Sears, Roebuck and Co., that "no person is so much in the backwoods as to be without the opportunity of buying everything imaginable."

The problem of clothing a family was much less complicated than it had been in earlier years. The lady who needed or desired to could order by mail all of her sewing tools, including the sewing machine and an assortment of fabrics and beautiful trim. Even hand-embroidered edgings and insertions were available, as well as cloth flowers and feathers for trimming a hat, beaded passementerie for decorating a fashionable, good silk dress, and cotton jean for sewing men's and boys' trousers. The supplies were endless.

In the 1880s, Lord and Taylor of New York circulated a catalogue and advertised in *Peterson's Magazine*: "Bridal outfits, ladies suits and underwear." Marshall Field published an issue with line drawings to illustrate the latest Paris fashions offered by the Chicago firm. These publications brought into

FIG. 67.—The first fashion illustration appeared in an 1878 Montgomery Ward & Co. catalogue.

thousands of homes a visual image of a way of life that could be conceived only through the "wish book." It became just that, especially for families on Texas' last frontier, the South Plains. One Montgomery Ward & Co. customer, Mary Moore Prideaux, recalled: "When I was a child, the arrival of Ward packages was like having Christmas come three or four times a year." The catalogue provided an exciting game of "You think of it, *Wards* has it."

With the first catalogues in the 1870s, the world of fashion took on a new dimension, although the selection of ready-made garments was limited.

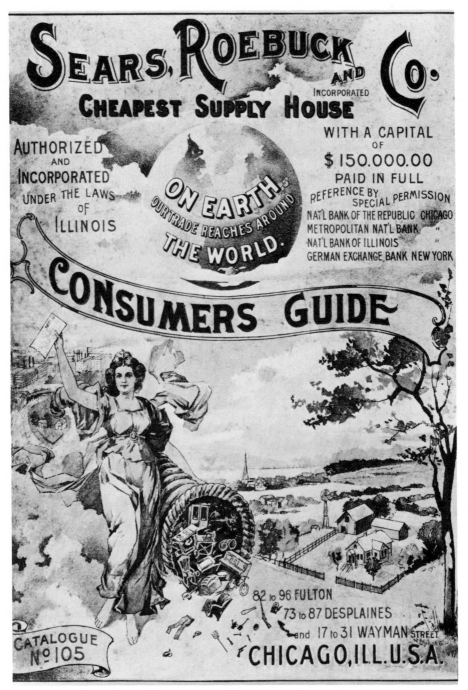

FIG. 68.—Sears, Roebuck & Co. catalogue of 1895.

FIG. 69.—Ladies' tailor-made suits were advertised in an 1897 Sears, Roebuck & Co. catalogue.

Wannamaker's of New York attempted to offer mail order service in the 1870s, and Cooper and Conrad of Philadelphia attempted it in the 1880s. They used periodicals such as *The Youth's Companion and The Farmer's Review* to advertise their merchandise. The competition in the mail order business that had developed by the 1890s made prices reasonable and merchandise offerings multiple. Almost every article of feminine attire could be ordered ready-made.

Once illustrations, like those included for the tailor-made suits from Sears, became available (Fig. 69), hardly a woman could resist ordering by mail.

In reaction to the competition, tailoring firms began to insert advertisements in women's magazines, many of them downgrading the so-called ready-mades. Free catalogues were offered through *The Delineator* by The National Cloak and Suit Company. They dealt with mail orders exclusively, and promised "everything made to order—Nothing Ready Made." Suits were nominally priced at $10 to $40, with the firm paying express charges to any part of the United States. Schlesinger and Mayer of Chicago prestigiously claimed to be "The High Water Mark Mail Order House of America."

Mail order houses sometimes promised Paris fashions, as in the case of Stern Bros., who stated, in an 1890 issue of *Cosmopolitan* magazine, that they gave

> direct attention to their weekly importations of Paris Costumes, wraps, bonnets, hats, and lingerie from the leading Paris Modistes, which with the production of our own workrooms enables us to offer at all seasons the largest and choicest collections to be found in the city. . . . Orders and inquiries receive immediate attention.

Part of the appeal of ordering a toilette made-to-order, a wrapper ready-made, a suit for the man of the house, and new dresses for the girls, was the excitement of receiving a package through the mail. A winter or summer list was made out for the family. Mrs. Clayton Carter, in a tape entitled "Early History of Lubbock," recalled, "It was a great event the day the huge packages came in on the mail hack, and everybody began trying on to see how their clothes fit."

MAKING A DECENT APPEARANCE

The women of the Texas frontiers were said to be "remarkable women in any sphere" (Holley, 1836). In addition to their willingness to rise to unspoken challenges, they also had a compelling need to dress so that they made a decent appearance. Any lady was expected to clothe herself and her family respectably; it was an unwritten index of character.

The *Ladies' Hand Book* declared in 1844: "The female who is utterly regardless of her appearance may be safely pronounced deficient in some of the more important qualities which the term 'good character' invariably implies" (Kidwell, 1979).

PUTTING ON THE STAYS

In keeping with the aim of respectability, there were prescribed and necessary garments to be worn, beginning with the underpinnings, which were modestly referred to in *A Little Book of Happy Thoughts*, of an anonymous author, located in the Museum library:

> Women ought every morning to put on
> The slippers of humility,
> The shift of decorum,
> The corset of charity,
> The garters of steadfastness
> The pins of patience.

Basic for the foundation of the unmentionables was the chemise, a long, loose garment (usually with brief sleeves) worn under the petticoats and corset, next to the skin. It was originally semi-fitted; by mid-century it was widened, had gathered gussets set in the front, and became rather voluminous (Fig. 70). Made of fine linen, lawn, muslin, or homespun, it amounted to a bodice and petticoat in one piece that reached below the knees. It was affectionately referred to as a "shimmy" and subsequently was decorated with fine punchwork embroidery and buttonholed, scalloped edging. Fine needlework graced even the most ordinary chemise.

Under the chemise the women and girls wore pantaloons or pantalettes in the 1830s that were made with wide tube legs trimmed with ruffles and lace. The trimmings were important because they showed under the skirt, which then was not floor length. Even when the skirt length was lowered to sweep the ground, particularly at the time of the hoop, the pantalettes continued to be fancifully trimmed because a glimpse of them was sometimes revealed under the full gowns when the ladies walked. After the 1860s it was not so necessary to emphasize their beauty because skirts were so full that there was little danger of revealing the pantalettes, so they were plainer, gathered below the knees with tight bands and came to be called drawers.

The corset, its early version known as "stays," was worn over the chemise and pantalettes. It was shaped with gussets at the breast and hips and was

FIG. 70.—The chemise (shown on figure) was the most generally worn of all undergarments. Pantalettes appeared only until the 1860s.

stiffened with boning, cane, or whalebone. The fitting of the corset was accomplished with back lacing. By the 1850s it was shorter, more shaped, and boned with whalebone, metal, or wood, and it hooked in the front.

"Putting on the stays" was the subject of many caricatures. A tiny waist was so much desired that even young girls were laced into these strictures. A mother had her daughter lie face down on the floor; by placing her foot in the small of the young girl's back, she could get the leverage to tighten the laces on the corset, thus diminishing the size of the waist. Eighteen inches was not a fantasy of waist measure—garments in The Museum Collection attest to that fact—but neither was it an ordinary measure.

Women and girls alike were willing to suffer in an effort to attain the tiniest waist possible. The story is told of a young lady who purchased a new silk gown for a ball in San Antonio when the state was still a territory. The dress was so snug that she needed a corset for the very first time in her life. The misery of the tight corset was so great that several times during the evening she sought escape to her bedroom to remove the corset so she could "catch her breath" (Brown, 1972).

The frontier lady may not have followed the extreme of corseting, but Victorian modesty nevertheless required that she wear one for special occasions. In mid-century the corset was sometimes adjusted and laced while damp to ensure a snugger fit. Women above the age of fifteen donned the corset as something of a holiday luxury. A general store owner recounted that the female members of his customer's families could be determined by the number of corsets ordered in the spring (Clark, 1964)!

The corset held an important place in milady's wardrobe from the 1830s until well into the twentieth century. It was one of the first ready-mades available to women and was being advertised in the 1860s to give form to the shapeless and charm to the graceless (Fig. 71). By the seventies a young adolescent could be outfitted with a "Darling," "Little Pet," or "Young Ladies' Beauty." A woman could order a seductive "Primrose Path" or "A La Spirite," which was awarded a gold medal at the Paris Exposition in 1889. It boasted a saucy flexible hip and could be had for $1. Warner Brother's "Health Corset" claimed to be comfortable while giving an elegant form. It was available in white or drab duck for $1.25 in the 1870s. There was Thomson's "Glove-fitting" corset, and Dr. and Madame Strong's "Celebrated Tricora Corset" in the eighties, and "The Venus, the very latest improved French Corset," of Zanella Cloth—all of which were available by mail order. The "Admiral Dewey," offered in the 1890s, ingeniously claimed to be a health corset: "its shape was a swirling twist which gave it the grace of Lillie Langtry and ruggedness of Calamity Jane, . . . the most perfect fitting health corset on earth" (Clark, 1964).

So important was this part of the wardrobe that in *Talks upon Practical Subjects*, as recorded in 1895, Marion Harland stated:

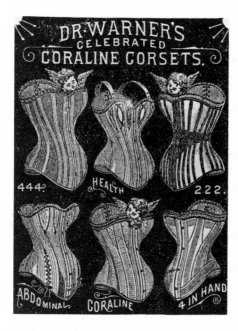 

Fig. 71.—Corsets were demanded by Victorian standards and were readily available by mail order by mid-nineteenth century.

> Women will wear corsets, they always have and they always will. We may well consider this
> a settled fact. There are good and sufficient reasons why they are a necessity to the women
> who dress as civilized women have for the past two hundred years. [Kidwell and Christman,
> 1974]

A practice of such long standing is not easily abandoned; the demise of the corset did not take place until long after the turn of the century.

While corsets changed little in style for most of the latter part of the century, the chemise was eventually shortened to the waist, the sleeves were eliminated, and it became known as a corset cover. Later known as a camisole, this garment was much lighter in weight than the chemise. The concentrated attention lavished on the beauty of its construction and finish is reflected in the satin stitch embroidery, drawnwork, yokes of tatting, crochet, ribbons laced through beading, or varieties of lace in combination that were used to trim the garment.

During the 1830s and 1840s as many as ten layers of petticoats were worn on top of the pantalettes, the chemise, and the corset, and they were made up of all manner of fabric. Wadded, quilted ones furnished both warmth and width, and also added bulk and weight. At least one red flannel petticoat was standard in the wardrobe of all women and girls. The number of petticoats required was reduced somewhat when crinoline was introduced in the 1850s. It was considered very progressive, because it took the place of two or three petticoats and was named for its content, the French term "crin," which means

NEW SKIRT for 1865.

J. W. BRADLEY'S
New Patent Duplex Elliptic (or Double) Spring Skirt.

  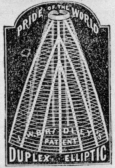

THE DUPLEX ELLIPTIC (OR DOUBLE) SPRING SKIRT is universally acknowledged throughout the LENGTH and BREADTH of the LAND to GREATLY SURPASS any Single Spring Skirt that EVER HAS OR CAN BE MADE, and is not EQUALLED in its WONDERFUL FLEXIBILITY and STRENGTH, its REMARKABLE LIGHTNESS, and NATURAL ELASTICITY EXPERIENCED in ALL CROWDED Assemblies, Railroad Cars, Carriages, Church Pews, Armchairs, Promenade, or House Dress.

IT will not BEND or BREAK, like the Single Spring, and consequently PRESERVES its PERFECT and BEAUTIFUL SHAPE more than TWICE as LONG as any other Skirt EVER MADE.

IT is the BEST QUALITY in EVERY PART, and UNQUESTIONABLY the MOST graceful and elegant as well as the MOST comfortable, economical, and durable HOOP SKIRT EVER OFFERED to the PUBLIC. For CHILDREN, MISSES, and YOUNG LADIES, they are SUPERIOR to all others.

THE HOOPS are all covered with TWO-PLY DOUBLE TWISTED THREAD, and WILL WEAR TWICE AS LONG as the single yarn covering which is used on all single steel Hoop Skirts. The three BOTTOM RODS on every SKIRT are also DOUBLE STEEL, and TWICE or DOUBLE COVERED, to prevent the COVERING from WEARING OFF the RODS when DRAGGING down STAIRS, STONE STEPS, etc. etc., which they are constantly subject to when in use. These SKIRTS also measure in circumference at the bottom from two and a half to four yards.

FOR SALE in all STORES where FIRST-CLASS SKIRTS are SOLD in THIS CITY, and THROUGHOUT the UNITED STATES and CANADAS, HAVANA DE CUBA, MEXICO, SOUTH AMERICA, and WEST INDIES.

AT WHOLESALE, by WESTS, BRADLEY, & CARY, PROPRIETORS of the INVENTION, and SOLE MANUFACTURERS, 97 *Chambers* and 79 and 81 *Reade Streets, New York.*

☞ INQUIRE FOR THE DUPLEX ELLIPTIC SKIRT.

FIG. 72.—Hoops, popular in the 1850s and 60s, helped to shape the full bell skirt and substituted for several petticoats.

horsehair, and "lin" from linen. The crinoline was fitted with pads or rolls of cloth to keep its shape. Eventually whalebone and reed, and then flexible bands of steel shaped into a framework, replaced the crinoline, and the hoop skirt made its appearance (Fig. 72).

When manufacturers were promoting the sale of hoops, commercially made with circles of watchspring steel riveted to vertical tapes to extend the petticoats, young girls in Bastrop County, Texas, found an ingenious way of making their skirts "bell fashionably." They set tucks in the under-petticoats and ran mustang grapevines through them, creating an effect almost as good as the commercial hoops. The skirt stood out full and tantalizing—an accidental flip could expose, of all things, not just ankles, but also legs (Carrington, 1975)!

The wearing of the hoops was not reserved for grown ladies, and it proved to be a great aggravation to many girls who had to dress up in style for special events. One little girl, dressed for a wedding in Tom Green County in the 1870s, wore a new blue silk dress with a hoop underskirt specially ordered from Philadelphia. Exasperated at not being able to sit without flapping the hoop up, nor to pull it down without it bulging at the sides, she slipped away during the ceremony, cut all the tapes, took the hoops to the woodpile, and attacked them with a hatchet. "I wrecked the hoops so badly there was no possibility of future use; then, like a punctured toy balloon, I went back to enjoy the wedding," she was quoted as saying (Green, 1974).

The bustle took over when the crinoline and hoops were abandoned in the late 1860s. The skirt fullness was moved to the rear instead of encircling the waist, and the bustle provided the shaping. It was made of a pillow or cushion of horsehair or a cage-like novelty of steel springs attached to a waistband. There was a myriad of styles offered, but the most commonly used was the pillow. One Texas lady used remnants of her Paisley shawl to fashion her bustle, which she stuffed with cotton. Others were made of muslin, silk taffeta trimmed with organdy ruffles, or just plain calico. Straw, cork, or wadding was used to stuff some of the bustles.

By Victorian standards women were required to wear numerous petticoats layered over the chemise or corset cover. Although one to three petticoats was considered necessary, even as late as the 1880s some women wore from four to six. Very few of the petticoats that survived the years are plain; most of them are trimmed to some degree, many of them elaborately so.

The mounds of undergarments that fashion and respectability demanded, as well as the embroidered trim for their making, could be purchased through mail order by the late nineteenth century. In 1881 Lord and Taylor offered cambric edging for purchase by the yard. Their catalogue stated:

> The perfection to which lace and embroidery has been brought by manufacturers places handsome underwear within the reach of all. . . . Good taste demands that all these garments should be made in dainty, simple styles, which may be easily laundered, the greatest care being taken to select fine cambric and delicate patterns of embroidery or lace.

But the fact remained that, even with purchased embroidered trim, there was still much handwork required to put it to proper use. In most cases, the top petticoat was fancy and the other layers were plain.

By the 1890s petticoats changed their shape, just as the skirts did. They fitted the figure more closely at the hips and were gored and belled into a flare at the ankles. Petticoats were frequently finished with flounces and ruffles that were tiered or layered, boasting row after row of fine tucking, insertions, hand embroidery, and other fancy trim. For dressing up, women favored silk taffeta, which made an impressive rustle. The story is told of women inserting newspaper in their skirts to simulate the sound of taffeta. The obsession with the rustling petticoat caused a writer for *The San Antonio Express* in 1899 to make this observation: "Petticoats are more tempestuous and persuasive than ever and who wouldn't scrimp and save to be able to rustle about in one of them." Young people of that time had vivid recollections of the pride with which their grandmothers and their mothers wore a silk taffeta petticoat when they dressed for special occasions. Even little children had fond memories of the fascinating rustle made when the ladies swished around in their long skirts.

"Sunday Best"

When families packed a wagon for the overland trip that would take them to a new land, they loaded it with necessities. Most of them also made room for a small trunk or bonnet basket that carried a few things for "Sunday best."

"Sunday best" was an expression commonly used to refer to frocks reserved for special occasions. A good black silk often served this purpose (Fig. 73). It might indeed be a lady's best dress for several decades; therefore, she kept it carefully stored away in readiness for those events that punctuated the life of the pioneer woman—weddings, church services, christenings, and parties. For some women, their good things were what they started with at the time of their marriage. Many young brides defied parents to marry and move west. Others came from cultured, highly social backgrounds, and started life on the frontier with a wardrobe saved from another way of life.

In spite of an uncertain future, a woman invariably brought with her something of the world she had left behind. In her log house one might find the elegance of tapestries and silver, and by the fireplace, a woodbox that was an Arbuckle's packing case. Inconsistencies were many in furnishings and dress. Reminiscences recall one lady on a ranch 100 miles from civilization, dressed as she had in England when she entertained at dinner: "Her black lace gown was by Worth. An engraved ruby ring, reputedly a stolen idol's eye, was but one of her jewels of historic lineage" (Cleveland, 1941). If her formality of dress and manner of serving appeared ostentatious, it was not deliberate; she had grown up to consider it an act of courtesy always to appear at her best.

A ball or dancing party called for something special and brought forth a variety of dress: a satin wedding dress, slightly altered; a Philadelphia debut ball gown of a decade past; a homespun linsey-woolsey; a silk gown created in the latest style by a modiste in Kentucky; or a calico made in the grand style of the moment. The same silk or cashmere frock often saw a lady through many seasons (Figs. 74, 75). When a special occasion arose, she could don her one good silk, and it made a difference in her outlook. As Ralph Waldo Emerson wrote in the late nineteenth century in *The Tattler Magazine*: "The consciousness of being perfectly well dressed brings a tranquility that religion is powerless to possess." Going to church services on Sunday was the only occasion some of the ladies had to show off a new dress and to enjoy a change from everyday garb. They yearned for the feel of silk, and their one "Sunday best" often served as traveling, party, and visiting dress.

Most of the best dresses, when new, followed the general mode portrayed in periodicals. In 1888 a feature advising women on dressmaking and the art of being well dressed appeared in *Arthur's Home Magazine*: "When you make

FIG. 73.—Black silk ensemble is made up in the style of 1876. It has black jet beading on basque and around bottom of polonaise, with pleated flounces encircling lower skirt edge.

FIG. 74.—Handmade plaid silk taffeta embodies features of the late 1830s or early 1840s, with piped seams, soft fullness in the bodice, and a skirt that measures 132 inches around.

FIG. 75.—This dress is made of silk foulard with black lace and ribbon banding. It is a truly elegant visiting frock of early 1890s that was worn by a rancher's wife in Motley County.

a new dress, let it be in the latest style so that it will look within the fashion for a longer time. Do not try to compromise." If a dress were made with this admonition in mind, selection of style and fabric involved much thought and was obviously a major decision.

GOOD FOR ANOTHER SEASON

The thrifty homesteader patched and darned for her husband and children, as well as for herself. Patches were laid on in such a way that many of them remain sturdy a century later. Examples that have survived reflect all degrees of sewing skills—some were carefully executed, some carelessly thrown together.

Even in this homely endeavor, women in the nineteenth century were encouraged to high achievement. An 1889 issue of *The New York Fashion Bazar* featured an article entitled "About Patching and Darning" in which the writer stated:

> The people in this world who get beyond the use of patches on garments are few and exceedingly foolish. . . . But not everyone is able to neatly lay a patch or darn a rent who might desire to do so, hence we advance a few helpful suggestions: In patching, start by cutting a piece of material of a size slightly larger than to completely cover the worn piece. Cut it accurately by the thread; nothing looks more untidy than a crooked patch with unshapely corners.

Extending the service of a good dress represented a positive challenge to many women. Clever methods were used for increasing the size, particularly the waist measure. Pleats were let out and gathering loosened, and an extension was added to the waistband and to the bodice opening. Waistlines were lowered, sleeves were redesigned, and new trim was added to give a fresh look to a dress fabric that was much too good to discard. Women were given this practical advice in an 1888 issue of *Arthur's Home Magazine*:

> If your dress is a wash dress make your skirt as full as the style admits of, for when you come to do any altering it is better to have it all look alike, as it certainly will not do if the piece is put away.

There are countless daytime frocks remaining in The Museum Collection that have been altered to provide for the changing shape of a woman's figure.

Catherine E. Beecher and Harriet Beecher Stowe touched on every aspect of homemaking in their 1869 book *The American Woman's Home*. One section devoted to mending made this suggestion:

> Silk dresses will last much longer, by ripping out the sleeves when thin, and changing the arms and also the breadths of the skirt. Tumbled black silk, which is old and rusty, should be dipped in water, then be drained for a few minutes, without squeezing or pressing, and then ironed. Coffee or cold tea is better than water.

Personal accounts of experience with a good black silk frock were recorded by ladies who admitted taking apart and remaking a dress several times. In the process they turned, sponged, dipped, French chalked, cleaned, trimmed, and altered until, as one woman stated: "It would have required vast ingenuity to do anything fresh to it."

By 1901 mending had become something of a science. The subject was dealt with in *The Delineator*:

> Twisting and turning, patching and piecing must continue to play an important part in domestic economy. . . . Old-fashioned people lament that the art of fine mending is lost. . . .

The old adage, "a stitch in time saves nine," like many other ancient bits of wisdom, has lost
none of its truth with the passage of centuries. It is just as well worth heeding as it ever was.

Making over a garment could try the skill of the most ingenious and patient
of ladies. However, if she remained undaunted by a sometimes meager supply
of goods, the lady on the frontier could make do with whatever was at hand,
converting the most unlikely thing into something wearable. A pretty dress
might be fashioned from a fine wool plaid shawl that had been in the family
a long time. An artistic lady might take an old India silk, the skirt of which
was slightly soiled and frayed around the bottom, and use it as a foundation
for a flounce from another dress and add a plait of new lace. By adding a
matching waist and sleeve trim, she would have a totally new look. Then, with
a coat of shoe polish and a few new flowers to revitalize her black straw
bonnet, she would have created an almost new ensemble for another season.

Complimented on her "new" black silk, one lady confessed (or boasted) she
had been wearing it for four years. She had freshened it by spraying it with
a teaspoon of ammonia mixed into half a pint of warm, weak coffee before
pressing it. Velvet cuffs, collar, pockets, and buttons had been made from an
old black velvet waist. Another industrious lady remodeled her black cashmere
after ripping it apart and washing it in warm water in which soap bark had
been steeped, then trimming it with a couple of yards of new silk. It was a
challenge to make something out of nothing, or to change its image by turning
it over, cutting it down, repatching it, letting it out, hemming it up, and
generally making do. From bits and pieces of silk and ribbons, fashion
neckties could be made. Embroidery and scraps of edging helped fashion
pretty collars and cuffs. Young girls' outgrown barred muslin dresses converted
perfectly into aprons with ruffles. Cream silk, said to wash as well as muslin,
was laundered and given a new frill of lace to make it appear in a new
character.

Many little girls wore coats fashioned from daddy's old coat dyed with
walnut husks. The upper pockets were dandy for mittens that were quilted on
the sewing machine, and pieces too small for anything else were stitched into
slippers. Mittens were also made from worn stockings. Little girls' Hubbards
came from old checked gingham skirts. In the 1840s one woman made her
husband an overcoat from an old wool blanket. She then carded the leftover
scraps, spun these and knit the thread into comfortable socks (Pickrell, 1970).

The resourcefulness of many women is reflected in the following testimony
of one lady from 1887 issue of *Arthur's Home Magazine*:

A lovely spring cloak was made a Mother Hubbard from an old drab, cloth dress. The
yoke was made of blue-shirred silk; the sleeves and skirt made of the cloth; large, hand-
painted buttons, also from an old dress, were used. Blue ribbons, two inches in width, were
secured to the side seams at the waistline, brought in front, and tied in a double knot.

This same lady had a good fur cap that she covered with drab cloth to match
the dress, and trimmed it with shirred satin. The fur was not damaged so that
when winter came she was able to return it to a winter ensemble.

Someone went to great lengths to enlarge the plum silk brocade dress shown in Fig. 76. Black satin panels were inset on each side of the bodice front and a matching brocade panel widened the back. A length of ivory silk faille was machine stitched over the buttonholes on the front opening—all combined to add a generous eight-inch expansion. All the back pleating had been released in the skirt and an extension was added to the waistband. The dress then possibly served for another season. However, it is evident that the remodeled dress was worn very little, which indicates that the remodeling may not have been successful. The manner of piecing and extending made it relatively simple for museum personnel to unpick the alterations and return it to its former petite size. Worn originally in Texas in the 1890s, it surely was the work of a modiste. Fine dressmaking details fashioned it, but the remodeling was that of a novice.

Although many garments remaining from the frontier ladies show evidence of having been altered, it is not always possible to discern the exact degree of changes that have been made. Sometimes it appears that changes were accomplished by degrees. The green wool challis shown in Fig. 16 had the waistline lowered by means of a pieced extension and the waistline enlarged by release of gathers in the skirt and bodice. It is logical to presume that it was more customary than unusual to get many seasons' wear from one good dress. The fact that there is anything at all left of these garments is a testimony to the excellence of fabric and the guarded care they were given.

DUST IN THE BALANCE

The limited wardrobes for everyday wear posed no special problem to the pioneer ladies who, with weekly regularity, did the household laundry. Washpots, rubboards, lye soap, bluing, and clothes lines were universally used for routine laundry chores, but caring for the good silks and especially nice things presented a challenge.

In nineteenth-century England and in the eastern United States, special garments were sent to a scourer for cleaning. Out of touch with the outside world as the homesteaders found themselves, there was no such convenience. Probably the most important thing the women did to keep their good gowns looking fresh was to guard their wearing. An important precaution was the wearing of dress shields, many of which have never been removed from the period garment. Reserved just for special occasions, a good dress was donned at the last minute and removed and packed away when not being worn. First, however, it was carefully dusted, with spots or stains receiving immediate attention. Laundering hints were passed on from one generation to another. Cold water, it was believed, could do no harm to any washable material; it removed stains better than any other agent and was recommended to be tried first. The colorfastness of calicoes could be tested by soaking the material in a mixture of a pailful of water and a teaspoon of sugar of lead.

FIG. 76.—Elegant dresses like this plum brocade and black satin costume suit of 1893 were made to last for several seasons. Details of workmanship and styling mark this as a modiste's creation.

For washing lawn or thin muslin, two quarts of wheatbran were boiled for half an hour in six quarts of water. After the water was strained, the garment was washed in the water with very little soap, and then rinsed lightly in "fair" water. This preparation was said to cleanse and stiffen the lawn without the addition of starch. If convenient, it was suggested that the skirt be ripped from the waist before ironing (Harland, 1886).

An 1865 issue of *Godey's Lady's Magazine* reported that scorch stains could be removed by laying the garment where the bright sun would shine directly on it. Worn spots on a gown or the shine on shoulders and elbows were freshened with the gentle friction of emery paper and then rubbed with a warmed silk handkerchief. Alcohol and strong whiskey would remove the stain of oil, wax, resin, and pitch, generally without removing the color.

Cashmere, a favored fabric for good dresses and children's things, required special care. If garments were lightly soiled, *Arthur's Home Magazine* recommended the following popular method of cleaning:

> Heat some flour in the oven, and with this rub every part of the material. Afterward brush out and shake the flour, and if any spots remain, repeat process. If the rubbing be carefully done, the gown ought to look new once more. . . . If very dirty, hand over to a professional cleaner.

Black cashmere was cleaned by washing it in hot suds to which a little borax was added. Rinsed in water made very blue with bluing, then ironed while damp, the fabric took on a surprisingly new look.

Sheer white things, considered too frail for regular starch, were dipped in milk, squeezed firmly, and pressed while still damp. This technique gave them a crisp, fresh look and was not considered as harsh to the fabric as starch. Weak coffee brushed on the rusty folds and worn edges of a good black silk would eliminate the rusty look that black so often assumed with age. One method of coping with velvet that had become crushed and shiny was the use of steam, created by lowering a hot iron held by a rope into a pail of water. With the crushed spot held over the rising cloud of steam, it was brushed briskly with a clean whisk broom, which lifted the nap and revived the velvet.

Bonnets were wrapped in an old handkerchief with the strings and lace straightened and rolled out. Most ladies took special care of their ribbon bows by wrapping the upper part of the ribbon with white paper to prevent it from becoming limp and creased. When one side was soiled, the ribbon could be turned so that the visible side appeared fresh and new. A bow of ribbon pinned to the neck or shoulder of the dress or in the hair added a special accent to even the most ordinary dress. No matter how ordinary her clothes or how rough her task, nearly every woman wore a bit of ribbon.

Devices for keeping the garments fresh were rather inventive. Few of the pioneer ladies had access to dry cleaning facilities until the turn of the century. Still, the garments in The Museum Collection are, for the most part, evidence of the pride with which the women cared for their special dresses and for the wardrobes of their families.

HOMEMADE BEAUTY

Through the annals of time, most women have been concerned with trying to make themselves more attractive. *Godey's Arm-chair* offered a bit of philosophy on the subject in 1870:

> It is not sufficient to say that ladies ought to be satisfied to appear as nature pleases, and that any attempt at embellishment deserves to be frustrated. In all ages, women and even the sterner sex, have been more or less rebellious against the sway of time. Early Asiatic races were well versed in the use of cosmetics, and the number of such preparations used by Roman ladies was very considerable.

On the Texas frontier at about the time this statement appeared, women were definitely interested in beauty, even though it might be home cultivated. Believing in prevention as an effective cure, they protected the face and arms from getting freckles or a tan by wearing large sunbonnets and by cutting the feet off of long stockings to slip over the arms. Then they bleached any freckles with buttermilk and salt and pinched their cheeks for a bloom.

Beauty suggestions were welcomed and the women longed for toilet articles. In 1865 a modest advertisement appeared in *Godey's*, the accepted adviser on all women's needs:

> The ladies' Toilet Vade Mecum: Containing full and complete directions for manufacturing all the requisites of the toilet, including Extracts and Perfumes for the Handkerchief; Pomades, Oils, Dyes, and Washes for the Hair; Lotions, Powders and Pastes for the Teeth; Creams, Balms, Rouges, and Beautifiers for the Skin; Scented Waters and Spirits, Perfumed Soaps, Lip Salves, Odorous Vinegars, Sachets, etc. By Laura K. D'Unger. Mailed free to any address, on receipt of 60 cents. Address Barry Percy, Box, P.O. Philadelphia, Pa.

Surely, this offer could answer almost any lady's beauty needs. Still, most of the women on the frontier had to make-do with what they could concoct. The "World's Fair Premium Face Fluid" recipe was one of these treasures. The recipe included 1 pound of flake white, 1 grain of carmine, 2 ounces of glycerine, 2 drams of rose water, 2 drams of bergamot, and 1 gallon of rain water. It was found in the memorabilia of an early pioneer on the plains, and claimed to make your skin as white and tender as a baby's. Beauty hints were shared back and forth, of course, and there were countless formulas and hints for beautiful skin, how to lessen wrinkles, and all sorts of miracle treatments.

A great deal of attention was given to the hands, inasmuch as white, soft hands were much admired and sought after. Mrs. Clayton Carter, in a tape entitled "Early Lubbock History," tells of some of the tricks used to produce white, soft hands. A simple trick for whitening the hands was to spread the inside of a pair of gloves with two tablespoonsful of oil of sweet almonds, one dessertspoonful of tincture of benzoin, one tablespoonful of rose water, and the yolks of two fresh eggs, and wear the gloves every night! Another trick was to cover the hands at night with cold cream, dip them in oatmeal flour or bran, and then cover them with gloves. Oatmeal water was advised for use after washing dishes. It was prepared with one pint of boiling water poured over one-half cup of oatmeal; when cool the mixture was strained through a sieve and used as a lotion. Another hand lotion was a combination of fresh lemon juice, rubbing alcohol, and glycerine.

For the woman who spent a great deal of time out of doors, care of the complexion was an endless challenge, especially since soft, fair skin was desired. Beauty packs were made of buttermilk and oatmeal, or an egg combined with warmed honey, lemon juice, and enough oatmeal to make a paste. In the fresh fruit season the addition of crushed strawberries, strained through a muslin cloth, gave the pack a special quality, as did the use of cucumbers that were boiled to a pulp with the skin on and strained, then added to the beauty treatment.

Cornmeal mixed with lemon juice, spread over the face and allowed to dry, was a special cleansing agent. Glycerine added to pure water in rinsing the suds from the face was said to do more "to beautify the complexion and preserve it smooth and clean than all the cosmetics in the world," according to Mrs. Clayton Carter.

Many women had a good cold cream formula that they swore by. One such formula was a combination of sweet almond oil and cucumbers, simmered four to five hours, then strained and mixed with white wax, spermaceti, and lanolin. Ingredients were then heated until melted, tincture of benzoin was added, and the mixture then was beaten with an egg beater until cold. An honored recipe for lessening wrinkles was a combination of wool fat, white wax, olive oil, camphor gum, and spermaceti. Some ladies recommended glycerine and rose water and a dainty film of almond oil on the face before applying powder. Rice powder was a favorite remedy for a shiny nose (E. J. Vickers, personal communication).

Believing that beauty came from within, women routinely took a spring medicine that consisted of powdered sulphur, cream of tartar, and molasses. One tablespoon of this mixture was prescribed for three mornings, omitted for three mornings, and followed by three more regular doses. For generations this sulphur and molasses mixture was considered a good body conditioner.

There were everyday, practical things that were believed to be beauty aids. About the time of the Civil War, young girls in the Bastrop, Texas, area were setting gourd bowls under the drip of the cut muskrat grapevine to catch the sap. They believed that washing their hair in the sap made it grow luxuriantly long (Carrington, 1975). A special treatment that promised beautiful and shining hair was the white of four eggs, beaten to a froth, and rubbed into the scalp. When dry, it was washed out with a mixture of equal parts of bay rum and rose water. To liven up, cleanse, and invigorate the scalp, and make a new and fresher hair growth, a mixture of one ounce of sulphur and one quart of water, shaken repeatedly every few hours, was used to saturate the head every morning. In a few weeks, the hair was supposed to become silky and lively, like a "clean baby's." This recommendation had been made by a city doctor, and the promised benefits sifted down to the frontier. The user was assured that sublimed sulphur was entirely insoluble, and the liquid would have no taste, odor, or color. In lieu of any of the formulas previously mentioned, a resourceful girl would combine castor oil and pine whiskey scented with lavender. Ingenuity and daring appeared to be the originator of many of the popular beauty hints.

For highlighting the hair, women learned that walnut stain gave it a rich brown hue; black tea also was successful. The blonde, who knew that she should wash her hair frequently, added bicarbonate of soda in the rinse, which was said to keep the hair fair and fluffy.

Curls could be coaxed by rolling the hair on kid leather curlers or curling irons that were heated over the chimney of a lamp. Some girls learned that the slate pencil heated in this manner was equally effective. For conditioning, they saturated the hair with one-fourth cup of olive or castor oil and one-eighth cup of glycerine. Lemon was considered a good rinse, or bluing, for gray hair. Witch hazel or boiled flax seed made a good hair setting lotion.

In the 1890s women kept hair receivers (little covered dishes with a hole in the lid) in which loose hair and combed-out tangles were hoarded. This extra hair could be shaped into a "rat" to help pad the pompadour, which was the full, brushed-up hair style much admired at this time. They also used a contraption much like a large tea strainer with a small hole in the back. The hair could be slipped through the hole, bent over and curled up into a turban-look. Available by mail were fake curls, chignons, buns, and waterfalls that could be pinned in place. Many women kept such hair pieces on hand to wear for the sake of style.

Women kept abreast of the latest hair fashion through illustrated periodicals. *The Cosmopolitan* in 1890 carried an advertisement offering a book of instructions on the "Modes in Coiffures," full of well-chosen and desirable illustrations of how to do a particular style, available for three stamps and mention of the magazine carrying the advertisement.

GOOD NEIGHBORS ALL

A hearty friendliness pervaded all of the Texas frontier from its earliest days. "Forget not to entertain strangers" was the happy admonition that frontier families took to heart. Any traveler, whether judge, schoolmaster, laborer, or peddler, was more welcome than a bag of letters or a file of newspapers. A guest came as a benediction, and everyone made an effort to make him feel welcome. An anonymous wayfarer recorded his experiences in the 1830s in *A Visit to Texas being the Journal of a Traveller*:

> Every well behaved stranger, on account of the news he brings, is a welcome visitor in such families as these, and this fact, in connection with the general prosperity of the people, and the kind dispositions of a large portion of them, renders their hospitality very sincere. To be received at the house of strangers with cheerfulness and pleasure, and welcomed with every favor in their power, is doubly agreeable when you feel that your society is regarded as a rich reward for all you receive.

The only social qualification required of a guest was good conduct.

Whatever her lot, the lady of the house was eager to share her board with others. In lieu of extra beds, which were rare, pallets of quilts and coverlets were spread on puncheon floors of the house or the dogtrot between the two sections of the double log cabin. Family fare could always be extended to accommodate the traveler—whether neighbor or stranger. Sometimes it was nothing more than venison, coffee, and biscuits, but it was presented freely, not necessarily "with the requirement and courtesy of a polished European community, but with the honest, blunt but hearty welcome of a Texas backwoodsman" (Holley, 1836).

Many women entertained in the old Southern tradition, which meant that the home was always open to any guests, invited or uninvited, a virtue of hospitality that earned for the people on the Texas frontier the label of good neighbor. So widespread was the feeling of welcome that it was not uncommon for a family to find a note upon their return home: "I came and you were gone. I ate a cold snack and then went on" (Pickrell, 1970).

The arrival of new neighbors, even if they lived thirty miles away, was heralded with acknowledgement. On hearing of their coming, folks hurried to have a meal soon on the scene. It was customary to send over butter, eggs, and a chicken. The gift might be accompanied with a request for some coffee or sugar in exchange, inasmuch as the settlers presumed that the newcomers had arrived with staples that were in short supply to those who had been settled awhile. Everyone, it was assumed, was willing to share with enthusiasm.

Little transpired among the neighbors that was not shared—events of joy or sorrow (Fig. 77). Many women would leave their families to fend for themselves while they answered someone's need for assistance during childbirth or an illness in the family.

FIG. 77.—The welfare of a neighbor was of concern to everyone, as is shown in this photograph.

When a neighbor or relative gave birth to a child, Rozalie would serve as a midwife. This was about the only visiting she did. Generally she took a length of calico to the baby's mother as a gift. [Carrington, 1975]

Some women were known to give up cherished trousseau items to furnish linen for a new baby's christening dress. Whatever they had was meant for sharing. The closeness of the people, bound with mutual concern, were fruits of special neighborliness in spite of the miles that separated them.

A QUEST FOR DIVERSION

Not surprisingly, one of the earliest cravings of the settlers on the frontier was for neighbors. There was a strong tendency on the part of settlers to encourage others to join them in community development, especially if the nearest neighbor was 100 miles away. Eagerness to make the newcomer feel welcome resulted in a multitude of "bees" that became popular gatherings. First, and logically, were the "sod house building bees," "log rollings," and "barn raising bees" to help a family plant its roots. The sense of celebration that characterized these creative events made them as much sport as labor. There were "house warming bees," "cornhusking bees," "quilting bees"—almost any occasion could be turned into some sort of "bee." While the men joined the work efforts, the women in their freshly done-up calicoes and bonnets got acquainted as they spread out the generous and tempting picnic specialties brought by all the neighbors. The day progressed with the children frolicking

FIG. 78.—Properly attired in riding habits and hats, these young folks are on a wolf hunt, somewhere on the Texas plains. (Photograph from collection of The Museum, Texas Tech University.)

FIG. 79.—Rabbit hunting was a popular diversion in Yellow House Canyon in the 1890s. (Photograph from collection of The Museum, Texas Tech University.)

while the women exchanged recipes and fashion news and discussed any gems of information gathered from newcomers who had recently arrived from the outside world.

During the Republic (before Texas' statehood, 1845), a quilting was on the order of a "log rolling": neighbors were called in to help do work that required many hands. After the pieces were assembled, a coverlet had to be quilted with tiny stitches following the intricate path of its design markings. Men assisted in the project by rolling up the quilt frames when it was necessary. They were expected to pass the thread and scissors and to entertain the workers with anecdotes and small talk, because the quilt had to be finished before the fun began. Then the supper, which had been cooking all day, was served—turkey, pork, cakes, pies, eggs, butter, milk, and preserves. When the fiddler took his place, it was the cue for the dancing to begin, and it might continue all night (Schmitz, 1960).

The pieced quilt, often made from worn-out garments, became an object of prime importance. It required so little in expenditure for the benefits it offered against the biting winds and bitter blizzards that howled outside the pioneer cabins. It was a thrill to a child to find a piece of a familiar garment worked into the design—like the small boy who proudly pointed to a tiny square to boast: "Them's me pants."

Quiltings and apron hemmeries helped many a young woman fill her hope chest in readiness for an upcoming wedding. As the country became more settled, quiltings were more of a ladies' affair. When a woman managed to get several quilt tops pieced from the scraps of goods left over from her year's sewing, she carded the cotton and ordered the lining or pieced it out of sugar sacks or "Bull Durham" sacks that had been ripped apart and sewn together again (Carrington, 1975). Then she set up the quilting frames, prepared a big dinner, and invited the neighbor women over to help with the quilting. The prospects of a good dinner and the opportunity to gossip and visit all day brought a happy response. Three or four quilts might be completed in a day. Not only was this gathering productive, but it offered an interval of respite from the routine, and women returned home richer.

Another dual-purpose diversion was hunting. Wolf and coyote hunts and buffalo and deer hunts all allowed parties of young people, chaperoned by married couples, to ride out and camp for two or three days (Fig. 78). In addition to supplementing the winter supply of food, these events provided an exciting time as well (Fig. 79). Newcomers on the prairies were stimulated with the thoughts of seeing buffalo that roamed in large herds in the 1870s and 1880s. One officer's wife wrote soon after reaching the fort: "Just imagine what fun it will be to go on a regular wild buffalo hunt. The ladies here all go on such things and enjoy it" (Green, 1974).

Candy pullings cemented many friendships and filled otherwise lonesome evenings. One batch of taffy could provide hours of flirting, fun, and fellowship! Countless courtships were begun in just this way.

Fig. 80.—Watermelon feasts went with summertime, and they were dress-up affairs. This happy gathering was in Eastland County around the turn of the century. (Photograph courtesy of Bill Green.)

FIG. 81.—Bonnets and buggies were a part of most picnic scenes, like this one at Buffalo Lakes in the 1890s. (Photograph from collection of The Museum, Texas Tech University.)

FIG. 82.—Picnics and fishing went together wherever there was water to be found. (Photograph from collection of The Museum, Texas Tech University.)

FIG. 83.—This light, summer dress of printed lawn, combined with yellow organdy and Val lace insertion, was worn by a young girl on a ranch near Fort Worth in 1890.

Above all, people on the frontier loved picnics, getting together with well-filled baskets, meeting old friends, and making new ones in an atmosphere of genteel camaraderie. Outdoor get-togethers were popular and widespread throughout America, especially on the Fourth of July, but any occasion—a birthday, wedding, or christening—was reason enough for a picnic. Sometimes, for no particular reason, watermelon feasts were spontaneously organized in the middle of summer (Fig. 80). If there were water in the vicinity, folks would gather nearby, because water usually meant that there were trees and shade. Sometimes picnickers resorted to the edge of a canyon, as the group pictured in Fig. 81, or around a watering hole, as shown in Fig. 82. By twentieth-century standards, the picnickers were definitely overdressed, but, as a release from life's humdrum, a picnic offered an occasion worthy of one's best. Women wore crisp, fresh frocks or waists and skirts over a volume of petticoats (Fig. 83).

By the 1880s barbeques were often taking the place of basket picnics. These were particularly popular for Fourth of July and were frequently held on the courthouse square. Families might camp out for several days. In a community with enough resources there was a brass band, dancing, horse racing, shooting contests, burro racing, and even pink lemonade. Ranchers donated fat calves for barbequing, and the women made cakes and goodies, and everyone looked forward to an event punctuated with excitement.

The matter of what to wear was of great importance to girls and women of all ages. They were known to spend months in planning and making a new frock for a singular occasion that might be the most important social event of the season (Fig. 84). A lady needed the assurance of knowing that she could make a "right smart appearance." It might be another year before she would be in a position to socialize with so many people again.

Ice cream socials also were highlight events by the 1890s. Ice, purchased in 300-pound blocks at supply points 100 miles or more away, was wrapped in tarps, then brought in by wagon. Buckets of sweetened milk mixture were then plunged into wash tubs of crushed ice and turned back and forth by the bucket handles until frozen. It took one man to two buckets and four buckets to the tub to make the ice cream. As many as 300 people might have gathered for such a summer festivity (Conner, 1958).

Church services, of course, were more than just a spiritual experience—they brought people together. Because many areas depended on a circuit preacher, services were infrequent; however, if there were a church in the vicinity, services might be more regular and more bountiful. In any event, it was important for everyone to be dressed in their "Sunday best" (Fig. 85). Sunday singings started early in the morning and lasted the entire day, interrupted by dinner served on the ground. Crisp summer dresses, hair ribbons, and frivolous but useful fans combined to reduce the oppression of summer heat. Camp meetings attracted people from a wide radius. Families who looked forward to the event for months camped around the big tent that sprawled on the hot

Fig. 84.—Sheer crossbar lawn, printed with dainty clusters of pale yellow flowers, was used to fashion this frock that was made in Tennessee and brought to Texas in the 1890s.

FIG. 85.—Rust sateen and black cut velvet are combined in this dressy "toilet" of the 1880s. The black bonnet, worn by a ranch woman in the Albany area, is comprised of banding of unique braid, alternated with shirred chiffon and trimmed with satin. The dress was worn by an early settler in Terry County.

FIG. 86.—Families pitched tents for weeks at a time to attend a camp meeting in the summer.
(Photograph from collection of The Museum, Texas Tech University.)

prairie of some new village. This was the kind of religious influence that reached the greatest number of Texans, and many of them came prepared to camp out for as long as a month to six weeks (Fig. 86). With all its seriousness of purpose, there was a festive atmosphere with so many people gathered together, giving the women a chance to show off new frocks and to get ideas and patterns from companions.

Some of the communities had what they claimed to be a cultured class of people who enjoyed literary and dramatic societies that came to be called Thespian societies. Interest in both professional and amateur dramatics grew to be intense in the 1880s, so much so that even small towns built opera houses—sometimes the most imposing building in the community. Cultural organizations for the purpose of diversion and social elevation became popular. One group, the Farmer's Wives Society, had rules that required the ladies to wear a plain home dress. This was "to keep the meeting from becoming an advertisement of the latest styles in fashionable attire" (Holden, 1930).

One popular community activity was visiting, a recreation reserved particularly for the times when there was no pressure of work to be done. Neighbors visited neighbors, even though miles apart. It was not uncommon for a family of six to ten people to drive up in their wagon to spend the day (Figs. 87, 88), and the visit might extend to several days.

Fig. 87.—"Going Visiting," as recorded by artist Richard Petri in Austin, 1849. (Courtesy of Janette Long Fish.)

Fig. 88.—Here the Boles family crosses their ranch for a neighborly visit in Lubbock County in the 1890s.

More settlement led to greater community involvement as the neighbors got together in quest of diversion. In addition to the "quilting bees" and camp meetings, there were Saturday night socials, fish fries, and a wide variety of events thought up by the innovative folks on the frontier in an attempt to get people together. Clubs and societies were formed according to the needs of the community—sewing societies, emergency clubs, entertainment clubs, dramatic societies—the list was long. Benefit of the Baptist Church Parsonage Fund or some other worthy cause would prompt a musicale of local talent. Schoolhouse box suppers were another means of making money. Weeks were spent by the young ladies decorating the boxes to hold the picnic suppers of fried chicken, pickled peaches, deviled eggs, pickles, elaborate cakes, and pies. The men bid on the boxes and whoever won the box was privileged to spread the delicacies in the company of the one who prepared it. Not only were these dinners a clincher for fund raising but also provided a good opportunity for matchmaking. The eager young man managed to discover which box was made by the girl he most admired. All the women dressed in their prettiest, most becoming frocks, like the one shown in Fig. 89.

The first public school in Texas was opened in 1853 on the west side of the San Antonio River on the Military Plaza. As each community acquired its own school, a new pattern of entertainment opened up. "Spelling bees," public examinations, school exhibits, and school programs centered around the

FIG. 89.—Community entertainment, such as picnics and box suppers, inspired the need for a new frock, such as this one of serpentine-striped cotton with deep lace yoke, worn by a rancher's daughter in early 1900s.

children and their activities. Anything oriented to education received high acclaim and full priority with the frontier folks, many of whom had received little formal education. An important and attractive factor also was the social benefit of getting people together; furthermore, it was a reason to get dressed up.

Most of the diversions served to bind the good neighbors more firmly together and shorten the distance between them. They shared their entertainment, which in most cases was homemade. By the turn of the century, when the populace was more settled, they even shared fireworks. Neighbors notified each other when they were planning to shoot the Roman candles so they could get in the yard to see the display seven or eight miles away. New Year's Eve was celebrated with a double blast from the old shotgun. Shooting the anvil was another way of creating a bit of revelry (E. J. Vickers, personal communication).

IN THE SADDLE

There was hardly a woman on the frontier who did not become an experienced rider. In many cases, being able to handle a horse meant the difference between mobility and staying home. Mary Austin Holley astutely observed of women of the early Texas frontier:

> Delicate ladies find they can be useful, and need not be vain. Even privations become pleasures; people grow ingenious in overcoming difficulties. Many latent faculties are developed. They discover in themselves powers which they did not suspect themselves of possessing, and equally surprised and delighted with the discovery, they apply their labors with all the energy and spirit, which new hope and conscious strength inspire. [Holley, 1836]

So they mounted their horses, even shouldered a rifle, and met the challenge. Of course, modesty demanded that all decent women ride sidesaddle; yet it was no small feat to avoid the tangle of an enveloping skirt and slip one leg over the side prong of the horn. Therefore, women learned to perform nearly miraculous maneuvers on their horses.

There is no record of how Sara Ann McClure was dressed in the 1830s, but it was probably in a long, full skirt over many petticoats, possibly with a pair of her husband's knickerbockers worn underneath. At Boggy Creek, while riding in Gonzales County, she and her husband met a band of Comanche warriors. Faced with upright banks of mud and a twelve foot chasm between the marauders and escape, she "fastened her reins in the horse's mane, wrapped her arms around his neck and buried her spurs in his flanks. The horse vaulted into the air, landing with his forefeet on the opposite side" (Brown, 1972).

Riding habits that trailed to within one foot of the ground were the style, even though they caught on the thorns in passing. Most of these costumes were designed to accommodate the right knee and the saddle prong and still allow the skirt to cover the ankle (Figs. 90, 91). These skirts often were of wool melton, a blanket-weight wool, usually black. It was customary to pull

FIG. 90.—The navy wool serge riding suit (1870-1880) from the Austin area is trimmed with brown leather straps, has a tightly fitted basque, and a long skirt that is shaped to fit over the saddle horn and knee, yet still cover the lady's feet when she was mounted.

Fig. 91.—A lady was expected to ride sidesaddle in the all-enveloping skirt of the 1900s. (Photograph from collection of The Museum, Texas Tech University.)

the riding skirt over a good skirt to protect it from mud and dirt, even though some thought the custom quite impractical.

In the 1870s the young bride of a Texas Ranger made herself a "fine up-to-date riding habit which extended below the feet from half a yard to a yard." When she was perched on a sidesaddle, the skirt reached almost to the ground. On her first ride out, the skirt caught in the brambles and was torn so that it barely covered the feet. "It was more convenient, but it required great care not to expose an ankle, which would have been scandalous." In desperation she finally sent to Austin for a "hunting suit" made of heavy material (Roberts, n.d.).

The women did learn to cope with the impossible skirts. When they settled in Palo Duro Canyon in the 1870s, families had to take six months' worth of supplies with them. Some of the wives drove wagons from Colorado, and a few more daring ones traveled on horseback—one as far as 400 miles from Trinidad, the nearest source of supply (Barton, 1928). It was not at all uncommon for young ladies to ride horseback as far as fifty miles to attend a dance carrying a party dress in a flour sack tied to the saddle horn!

By the 1890s a riding skirt was designed that was full legged and divided like trousers, following the lead of Amelia Jenks Bloomer, who had introduced trousers for women, only to be ridiculed. A full-length panel that could be buttoned down the front when the lady dismounted made it acceptably modest. With the panel buttoned it resembled a skirt; worn with a matching

FIG. 92.—Women found this type of divided skirt and tailored jacket of heavy cotton twill practical because they could ride astride without embarrassment.

FIG. 93.—For many women and girls the riding outfit was whatever they happened to be wearing—in this case, a white shirtwaist, plaid skirt, and sunbonnet. (Photograph from collection of The Museum, Texas Tech University.)

tailored jacket, it made a very neat appearance (Fig. 92), and was frequently made up in a khaki-colored twill fabric, cotton, or wool. The sidesaddle was no longer required and women enjoyed the freedom of riding astride. No doubt there were those who disdained the divided skirt and clung to the standard skirt with petticoats, as shown in Fig. 93. There also was a class of the avant-garde who donned their husbands' jeans or overalls and disregarded the risk of criticism.

A PASSION FOR DANCING

Word would go round, somewhere, anywhere, on the Texas frontier, that there was to be a dance. "Come one, come all" was the welcoming invitation. People would come from as far away as fifty miles for the dance that might last from sundown to sunup, continuing for two or three days on occasion. They had a real passion for dancing (Figs. 94, 95), and their dancing was like their lives: "all full of earnestness and energy—vim was an element in everything here then" (Carl, 1937), were the recollections of an early Texan! A dance might take place on the hard dirt in the moonlight to the rhythm of a guitar, harmonica, Jew's harp, banjo, or whatever musical instrument that could be had, or a dance might be a fancy dress ball.

As early as the mid 1820s, when Texas was still a part of the Republic of Mexico, Houston was the scene of grand balls where the ladies were beautifully gowned in costumes brought from the United States, dancing to the music of violin, cello, and fife in a ballroom lighted with sperm candles in wooden chandeliers. At the same time, there were dances in less elaborate settings. For wedding parties in the home of a bride's parents, furniture was moved out to make room for the guests. Music for dancing was furnished by several musicians with fiddles and possibly a pair of clevises used as cymbals, in celebration of the wedding bond signed by the bride, who might be no more than fourteen years old, and her groom (Schmitz, 1960).

Country dances, cotillions, and waltzes followed each other in rapid succession. In the very early years of the Republic, all sorts of occasions resulted in a dance or a ball—election affairs, barbeques, quiltings, weddings, and christenings. In the 1830s people got together for a triple occasion that included a barbeque, ball, and an election. The day was filled with activities: the ladies quilting, men throwing horseshoes, and the children playing. For the young folks, dancing might begin at three o'clock and last until the next morning. What the young women wore was often an unforgotten memory (Fig. 96). "Mother ripped up an old silk dress and made me a ball dress," was the reminiscence of one young girl (Schmitz, 1960).

Guests often came from miles around the country for a ball given in honor of a new bride. All the ladies came out in their best frocks. The bride might be dressed in pink silk with exquisite lace and superb diamonds. Even in a log cabin with rough hewn floors for a ballroom, there was silk and broadcloth side by side with calico and buckskin. Many such festivities came

FIG. 94.—Dances made up a part of most social gatherings in the early years of The Republic. (Courtesy of Culver Pictures.)

FIG. 95.—Ranch hands and women of all ages looked forward to the annual Christmas ball during Texas pioneer days.

Fig. 96.—This black silk of the 1840s is handmade. The pointed basque fastens down the back with hooks and eyes, and the full, flounced skirt is worn over many petticoats.

FIG. 97.—Pink silk brocade and pink taffeta are combined in this fashion of the early 1870s that was made in Michigan and brought to Texas by the daughter of a lumber merchant. It has assymetrical draping of the overskirt, trim of pouffs, shirring, and knife pleating. The buttons are crochet-covered iridescent balls.

to a sudden halt when an Indian raid caused the men to drop the hands of their dancing partners and seize their rifles (Hogan, 1947).

Even though their world was fraught with danger of Indian attacks, people grasped the slightest excuse for a celebration. Theological discourses that had held them spellbound "back in the States" no longer made folks sit and listen. A ball or dance answered the need, and these occasions brought out a surprising number of fine and beautiful gowns, some of which were bought in New York, Philadelphia, or New Orleans; others were made of silks ordered from England or France (Fig. 97).

A ball held in Houston in 1837 was the occasion for an elegant display of fashion. Francis Lubbock reported that "Ladies and gentlemen came on horseback distances fifty and sixty miles, accompanied by men servants and ladies' maids, who had charge of the elegant costumes for the important occasion" (Lubbock, 1950). Another account presents a picture of what people were wearing:

> Mrs. Baker's dress of white satin with black lace overdress, corresponded in elegance with that of her escort, and the dresses of most of the other ladies were likewise rich and tasteful. Some wore white mull, with satin trimmings; others were dressed in white and colored satins, but naturally in so large an assembly, gathered from many different places, there was great variety in the quality of costumes. [Schmitz, 1960]

One lady had a bouffant white velvet that she had brought from Kentucky. Another, Mrs. Yoast, wore a gown of buff velvet with a full skirt, a tightly fitted basque, and an elegant lace bertha. The dress and her splendid jewelry of amethyst and pearls were all a part of the wardrobe in which she had made her debut to Virginia society following her return home from Europe where she had been educated.

In 1847 Viktor Bracht wrote from "Spanish" San Antonio to friends and relatives in Germany:

> You are mistaken if you think that there is no luxury here. Women pay more attention to dress and finery in San Antonio than they do in New York, and in the large cities of Europe. We have balls and soirees. [Bracht, 1931]

Other reminiscences describe ball gowns as "notable for their elegance and artistic taste and skill evidenced in their design, blending of colors and construction." Some of the ladies appeared in green brocade, white satin, white brocade, white grosgrain, all "en train" with crystal, gold, diamonds, lace, and pearl trims. Some gowns were decollete. There were gowns of brown velvet with pink roses, pink ottoman satin, Elizabethan collar with passementerie trimmings, and amber satin with crimson plush and amber beads.

While the women seemed comfortable enough in their concern for what they wore, men sometimes suffered in their efforts to be correctly dressed, as indicated by one young man:

> Since the War, San Antonio has changed. Now it is necessary to have fine new clothes for every ball. The ladies are up in style, from studying the Bazar. And just think I had to buy a white satin vest for myself. It is not comfortable in this heat. After the day's work, and dancing the first polonaise and waltz, I have to sit with that vest on! [Chabot, 1940]

Later in the century the opera house was often the scene of the grand balls, especially in smaller cities. In 1891 a young belle ordered her wedding gown and her ball gown to be custom-made by Madame Sanders of Louisville, Kentucky, for her wedding in the remote area of Vernon, Texas. The wedding dress, made of robin's egg blue corded silk and trimmed with white ostrich tips (Fig. 98), and the trained coral silk faille ball gown both illustrate skilled, professional construction, surely equal to anything worn in the city. Both dresses served the blithe spirit of Miss Hattie Napier for her wedding festivities when she married Mr. Thomas Shive, inasmuch as she had a real fondness for dancing—a favorite pastime at the Opera House in this small Texas settlement. These two outstanding gowns are preserved in The Museum Collection.

Fashionable clothes worn to the galas were often described in detail in local papers. In the 1890s an Abilene newspaper reported many shirtwaists and skirts that were elegant and elaborate: black taffeta skirt with waist of white tinsel illusion, jewels of amethyst, pearls, diamonds, and garnets; a black brocade skirt with white crepon waist and pearl trimmings; black brocade skirt with waist of pink mousseline de soie, jet ornaments and diamonds; black crepon skirt, black jetted over-skirt with satin and holly at throat and in hair; black velvet with Dresden silk waist; black silk skirt and pink brocade silk waist with diamond ornaments. There were gowns of nun's veiling, chiffon, Albatross lace, Triplett white silk lace, mull over blue silk, salmon satin with diamond ornaments, white organdy over pink silk with roses and diamonds— a dazzling array of brilliant costumes.

Balls, parties, weddings, and other gala occasions were graced by both men and women dressed in their best attire. Styles usually varied according to the period in which the wearer had emigrated to Texas. The variety of gatherings ran a gamut from the hops or square dances and "calico hops" in the outlying communities to the fancy dress balls, masquerade balls, leap year balls, and other special invitation-only affairs. In rural areas, news got around by the mysterious grapevine, and to hear of a dance was to consider oneself invited.

Preparations for a dance were usually made well in advance and with great anticipation. Women wrote about wearing a new white organdy waist and fan chain, or a pretty pale blue "inspire." One girl had just gotten cute new slippers, and "beaded them in bowknots myself," for an upcoming dance. Best dresses were pressed, and hair was curled. If the trip must be made by horseback, it was just part of the adventure, because the chance for socializing was worth the effort.

Up in Style

Weddings on the frontier took many forms, took place in all sorts of settings, and were always events of great social importance. Weddings involved long preparations and promised a season of good fellowship. Engagements were announced several weeks, even months, in advance. Brides were very young, some only fourteen or fifteen years old, especially when the state also

FIG. 98.—This 1891 wedding dress of robin's egg blue, trimmed with ostrich tips, lace, and braid, was custom-made by Mme. Sanders of Louisville, Kentucky. The close-up shows construction details and labeled "petersham" (belt inside bodice).

was young. There seemed to be a passion for wasting no time in getting roots planted and a new world started. One young man observed in a letter written in the 1840s that he had been to a wedding: the bride "was not quite sixteen. Just a good age" (Chabot, 1940).

The exact date of the wedding was often determined by the unexpected arrival of the preacher, usually a Methodist circuit rider or a Baptist missionary on a regular circuit. The invitation was circulated by word of mouth until late in the century, when printed or written invitations became available and popular. Everyone within thirty or forty miles was included. If a young bride came from the east to join her youthful groom, who had arrived earlier to file on his land, the neighbors would handle the wedding festivities, which could, and often did, last several days.

Nuptials were performed wherever the space would allow—in the parent's sod house, a log cabin, an elegant home, or a church, if there were one near enough. On the plains, the vows were sometimes said on the porch, if the home were too small to accommodate all the guests. There were also buggy weddings during which the bride and groom remained seated in the buggy, with their friends and family standing nearby. The happy couple then drove away immediately after the ceremony (Connor, 1958).

Getting the marriage license was not always a simple affair, inasmuch as the groom might be required to ride 200 miles to get it. After the ceremony, the bride's father might take the bridal pair in a covered wagon to board the train for the honeymoon, which sometimes meant two days of hard driving.

FIG. 99.—So-called "elegant simplicity" is shown here in a jewel-trimmed silk taffeta two-pieced wedding gown of 1899, especially made for May Louise Matthews (Mrs. Thomas Lindsay Blanton).

Wherever and whenever, the wedding was a stylish an affair as could be managed, and the bride's dress, which might be the dress of her lifetime, deserved and received much attention (Fig. 99). In the early years, some brides spun the yarn to weave the fabric for their dresses. Others brought elegant gowns of silk from the east or New Orleans, or had them made up by a modiste in Kentucky or Fort Worth. Many gowns were fashioned by the mother or sisters of the bride, and were made of material bought at the mercantile or emporium, or ordered from the mail order catalogue. They ranged from formal, traditional white satin to simple cotton lawn, trimmed with ribbons and flowers at the neck and in the hair. Not uncommonly, the bride was married in a good dark dress or suit that was to be her best dress for years to come.

In the 1830s weddings were solemnized with all-night feastings. After "the bridegroom with the bride under his arm, supported by the necessary attendants, were brought before the minister," the "I wills" were pronounced. Then festivities usually continued all through the night (Schmitz, 1960). The first wedding ceremony in the Beaumont community was performed in 1832 in front of a blazing fire in the fireplace of a log cabin. The feast afterwards included venison, wild turkey, and ducks out of the backyard of the bride's parents.

Many courtships that resulted in weddings were started at camp meetings. In 1861, near the settlement of Cedar Hill, one young man announced to his friends that he would ask the girl who came wearing the largest hoop to sit with him. When a young girl in a bordered white lawn dress over hoops of breath-taking size stepped down from her wagon, the young man made his choice, and later that year the couple was married. She wore a gown similar to the one that had started the courtship, a full bell skirt over hoops and crinoline (Carrington, 1975).

Around the military posts the occasion of a wedding was a very elegant affair. Wedding cards were sometimes sent out, and the house might be prettily trimmed with evergreens. One bride was reported to be wearing light blue silk with a long white veil and orange blossoms in her hair and at her neck. Her bridesmaid was in white Swiss trimmed with cherry blossoms. Following a lengthy Episcopal ceremony the bride and groom received their congratulations, and then a hearty breakfast of bread, butter, coffee, two kinds of salads, turkey, ham, oysters, pickles, bride's cake, fruit cake, jelly cake, and champagne was served. An occasion so grand was of monumental note among the settlers, inasmuch as they seldom were witness to such a splendid event (Green, 1974). At about the same time in the 1870s, a young bride on a ranch near Albany, Texas, wore a white alpaca wedding dress made by her sister using the pattern supplement from *Harper's Bazar* as a guide (Fig. 55). A trousseau usually included a second-day dress, which the bride wore for the infare, a dinner in the home of the groom's family the day after the wedding. As her second-day dress, this little bride wore a grayish tan dress trimmed with blue collar and cuffs. She had personally covered all the dozens of little rice shirt buttons with blue silk to match the collar and cuffs (Matthews, 1958).

Blue seemed to be a favored color for the second-day dress. One young woman chose pale blue china silk, another a royal satin with tapestry-striped trim. Blue wool fashioned into a tailored suit was the choice of another bride, and blue and white embroidered striped novelty cotton was a pretty summer choice. These dresses are all in The Museum Collection, as are the wedding dresses referred to in the following account.

Many brides reported the luxury of having their wedding dresses especially made up by a French dressmaker in Fort Worth. White swiss, silk de chine with jeweled trim, or fine silk with spatchel lace and fancy brocades were choices of various brides. By the 1890s brocade satin was being ordered from Montgomery Ward & Co., and supplies were readily available from many sources for creating the gown for "nuptializing" and for the infare on the second day.

Off the caprock, where ranchers were becoming affluent, weddings punctuated the frontier world with class, and bridal gowns reflected this growing wealth. In the 1880s and 90s there were French-designed gowns said to have cost $500. One of satin marveilleux with silver brocade built on a princess foundation was special ordered through Sanger Brothers in Dallas, made by a famous modiste for a cattle baron's daughter in 1884. Another distinctive wedding gown was white silk taffeta trimmed with chiffon, seed pearl-beaded fringe, and swags of pearls down the skirt front panel. This dress, shown in Fig. 99, fits the connotation of elegant simplicity as interpreted in 1899 and was worn in a church wedding near Albany, Texas.

While the white wedding gown was appearing more often, there were, of course, many brides in Texas who, of necessity or choice, wore a pretty silk in a practical color. Among these practical dresses have been found a gold taffeta polonaise from the 1880s, a dark olive green faille with bronze beading and ciselé velvet from the 1880s, a plum satin with sculptured metal buttons, a sage green alpaca trimmed with lace and satin ribbon from the 1870s, a brown plaid silk taffeta with full skirt and bobbin lace collar from the 1860s, and even a light green silk skirt topped with a sheer white muslin blouse from the 1830s. Fortunately there is enough sentimentality attached to the wedding for ensuing generations to have guarded the survival and documentation of these beautiful gowns chosen by different girls in different parts of the frontier and the state over a long timespan.

POWER OF THE PRESS

Very early in the nineteenth century, newspapers began to go to press in scattered corners of the Texas frontier. Bearing a folksy tempo, familiar and intimate, they appealed to all readers, and the editor influenced his readers through editorial opinions and advice. Whether published weekly or less often, the area newspaper was chief reading material for most families, with the exception of the Bible and the mail order catalogue. The editor, who frequently was the only member of the publishing staff, realized the power he wielded. He performed, therefore, the roles of etiquette advisor, humorist, neighbor, philosopher, fashion dictator, and sometimes cynic. He challenged the people to "Go to church next Sunday. It can't hurt you and it might do you a lot of good."

The *Mason County News* printed the requisites of the well-bred girl in 1889:

> She does not talk loud in public places. She doesn't want to be a man. . . . She doesn't scorn the use of a needle, and expects some day to make clothes for very little people who will be very dear to her.

The editor waxed poetic for his advertisers, and no doubt he influenced the status of certain merchants with ditties like this one in the *Mason County News* in the 1880s:

> The ladies of Mason, bless their sweet lives,
> The radiant maidens and the good queenly wives
> Dress finer than any who dwell in the West
> Because Smith and Geistweidt sell them the best.

Publishers often took glee in poking fun at fashions. They went on the assumption that printer's ink could influence what the women wore. They filled their columns with comments and lamentations about fashion.

The Mother Hubbard or wrapper, the loose-fitting "at home" frock that was worn everywhere for a good many years (Figs. 36, 37), brought forth opinionated reactions. Critics claimed that its voluminous swishing skirt frightened horses, thereby causing serious accidents. Some writers suggested that no woman should be permitted to wear the wrapper without a belt. Others described it as being far too unbecoming and dangerous.

Even though the full hoop skirt had become an aggravation and the subject of ridicule, men did not think much more highly of the bustle when it supplanted the hoop and left long trailing skirts to drag behind. The editor of the *Houston Post* made this interesting comparison in 1885:

> It is hardly worth while to tell our fair friends that men do not admire the revival of long skirts and the hitching gestures which they entail upon women. Nature has given but one animal a train and that is a peacock. The bird is not compelled to kick its appendage into shape behind and therefore wears it gracefully.

In an attempt to refrain the women from letting their skirts swish around the ankles and trail on the floor, the editor of the *San Antonio Express* penned the following advice in 1899:

> One thing that will be good news to all women is that shorter dresses for the street will not only be tolerated but the smartest thing out. In fact, no fashionable woman appears in a gown that comes anywhere near touching the sidewalks, and what is best of all, you can choose your own length. . . .I expect some people will be shocked when they first see the short skirts and say they are not modest. They would rather go through the muddy streets with their skirts clutched up on one side until they make a display that would cause a ballet dancer to blush while the other side is heavy with mud.

Fig. 100.—Wedding gifts reached a high point of extravagance in 1900 and often were listed in the local paper with names of donors.

In spite of this tirade, fashionable women continued to wear long swishing skirts for many years.

Most of the men of the press could not desist from philosophy and advice. There is no question that they did influence attitudes and thinking. Their advice was often homely, character strengthening, or, to say the least, challenging. They addressed themselves to the men as well as to the women, as shown in the *Weekly Review*, published in Sweetwater in 1900:

It is the law of God. It isn't exactly in the Bible but it is written large and awful in the lives of many misfit homes. . . .If one of you chaps ever runs across a girl who, with her face full of roses, says to you as she comes to the door, "I can't go for 30 minutes yet for the dishes are unwashed," you wait for that girl. You sit right down on the doorstep and wait for her, because some other fellow may come along and carry her off and then you'll lose an angel. Wait for that girl and stick to her like a burr to a mule's tail.

The reader's health, both physical and emotional, also came under the editor's scrutiny. Long discourses were printed on the topic of keeping one's beauty, and the question was raised as to why so few women were able to do so. *Home and Farm* newspaper offered a solution to the lady who was never quiet for a moment or able to relax when the chance would come for a respite:

They go on using up their nervous systems until one day comes a grand collapse. . . . What if there is a speck of dust nestled away beneath some ornament or chair leg, what if there are some tasks slighted and some others left entirely undone, the house won't go to rack and ruin in consequence.

Beauty could only be achieved by cultivating repose, the editor preached, which was not an easy solution for a frontier lady whose days were programmed completely with things that had to be done for the very subsistence of the family.

The highlight of the news for a good many years was a wedding account. Much space was allotted to the bride, and the editor embroidered his most flowery language to equal the occasion. As a token of thanks, he was rewarded with a big cake with white frosting. "It became the written law of the land that every wedding 'written up' meant a cake for the editor (Holden, 1930)." The cakes became very elaborate to ensure a better story. Sometimes there was included in the paper an itemized list of the wedding presents, complete with names of donors (Fig. 100).

The following excerpt from *The Stockman*, published in Colorado City in 1900, describes a wedding in a young Texas frontier town:

THE WEDDING
"Love took up the harp of life,
And smote on all the chords with might."

It is an old and well accepted saying that "all the world loves a lover," and in the shifting panorama of these earthly scenes, there is scarcely an event of more universal interest than the union of two lives by matrimonial ties. Such, indeed, proved the case in this romance of two cities, blissfully consummated in Sweetwater last night. First, let it be mentioned that the interior of the Christian church in Sweetwater had been decorated in a manner so pleasing and beautiful, and in such entire consonance with the occasion as to richly deserve the admiration bestowed by the assemblage. The church was entirely filled with people awaiting the performance of the ceremony. Each aisle was spanned by two arches, composed of English ivy and white roses entwined with white and blue ribbons, the color theme of both the church and house decorations. The aisles were spread with white, leading to the altar, where there arose arches decorated after the same manner, together with a profusion of ferns and potted plants. It had passed 9 o'clock when a choir of six voices sang the bridal chorus, "Faithful and True." [Fig. 101]

The large bridal party was described in detail:

FIG. 101.—This pictures the setting of a turn-of-the-century wedding in Sweetwater.

[The bridesmaids were] all attired in airy white organdies, looking like veritable fairies from fairy land as they came bearing their rose chain, making an aisle for the bride and groom. Next came little Gussie Ragland as the minister's attendant, representing Cupid, bearing the marriage license in the gleaming bow and arrow, convincing proof that "love is but the fulfilling of the law."

Five of the attendants wore pale blue crepe de chine trimmed with appliques and chiffon, two were in white mousseline de soie over white taffeta, and the maid of honor wore embroidered chiffon over crepe de chine and a becomingly arranged veil. Doing justice to the bride, the editor described her in the following way:

[The bride was] superbly gowned in white duchess satin ornamented with real pearls and pointlace, carrying in her hands a beautiful bouquet of bride's roses. Her only jewel, the gift of the groom, was a diamond sunburst surrounded by pearls, fastening the filmy veil to her beautiful dark hair.

The reception, held in the home of the brother of the bride, included the ritual of the "loving cup," both bride and groom drinking from the double-handled silver goblet to ensure happiness. Monogrammed "dream" cake boxes tied with blue satin ribbons were presented to the guests to take home and place under the pillow to induce dreams of one's lover. The bride's traveling dress was a pastel shade of heliotrope, trimmed with cut pearls and steel buttons, with hat and gloves to match. Guests for this Sweetwater wedding had traveled from

FIG. 102.—Achieved at last on Texas' last frontier were spacious, elegant homes arising in testimony of the stability and affluence that was evident over all of this great state by 1909. This building has been restored on the site of The Ranching Heritage Center of The Museum of Texas Tech University. (Photograph from collection of The Museum, Texas Tech University.)

as far away as Kansas City, San Angelo, Fort Worth, and Abilene. Through the courtesy of the Texas and Pacific railway officials, a special coach was provided for the transportation of the Colorado friends of the bride and groom.

Of course, the luxury described in the account just examined was not typical of most weddings, but neither was it rare. By this time there were many families who could afford to and did make an elaborate affair of their daughter's wedding. The last frontier was being tamed and the lifestyle was changing for the people of Texas (Fig. 102). No longer were supply sources so remote. A new freedom was being realized, and for many the world was less harsh and afforded some of the niceties that could be had in the city.

THE LOOK OF LEISURE

As the new century was ushered in, Texas' last frontier was firmly established on the Llano Estacado. Even though many families who came later arrived by covered wagon, the trip was not as agonizing as it had been for others a decade earlier. The railroad was reaching into the outskirts of the state, and supplies were becoming more easily obtained; yet there was still a segment of settlers striving for subsistence. Contrasts with development in the metropolitan areas of the East and even in the southern and eastern parts of the state were dramatic.

It was 1909 before the railroad reached Lubbock, one of the last links to the industrialized world. Even so, side by side could be found the frontier lady in calico wrapper still struggling to keep her family clothed and the city dweller with store-bought garments or those made up by a professional dressmaker.

Within a short time, labor-saving devices were decreasing the work load for the woman of the house. Carpet sweepers for the rugs, gasoline irons to replace sadirons, and sewing machines to eliminate much of the tedious hand-stitching could all be had by mail order. Kerosene lamps meant that folks no longer had to make their own candles. There were kitchen sinks, ice boxes, and washers with wringers to ease the laundry work load. There were still many families boiling their laundry in the big black washpot and heating their irons on the kitchen stove, but, generally speaking, life was not so tedious as it had been.

Almost every item of clothing was available ready-made at moderate prices for each member of the family. Many women still preferred to make their own things, however, and many of them did so out of necessity. Wide selections of fabric and trim were easily obtained, and the sewing machine made clothing a family less of a chore than it had once been. Patterns and dressmaking guidance abounded in ladies' periodicals and home magazines. "There is one mental quality that is very important to the buyer of patterns," read *The Ladies World* of 1909, "and that is imagination." From the women, there was a continual cry of "Give us home dressmakers simple patterns," and many more firms and periodicals began to offer patterns and instructions.

Suddenly the new look that science, industrial development, and social and economic changes gave to almost every aspect of daily life rubbed off on fashion. The bustle had vanished by the end of the 1890s, and a new, slim silhouette took its place. There was an increased simplicity of style, even though it was far from plain. Fewer petticoats were worn, and skirts, except for evening wear and special occasion gowns, were clearing the floor. The advent of the automobile contributed a great impetus to the change in ladies' dress; mobility made possible by the horseless carriage necessitated more practical clothes. Education was becoming attainable for women, and girls were sent off to college. These college women were the style setters for the rest of the women.

From the 1890s on, there appeared a fondness for light colors, with white taking an important role (Fig. 103). By 1906 the mode of light, airy cotton fabrics for shirtwaists and dresses had become the rage all over America. The Edwardian women of fashion promoted this desire for elegant white frocks, all made by hand, as a mark of distinction. Soon, however, the style was copied in inexpensive ready-mades. Patterns and instructions became so readily available that women everywhere adopted the look of leisure (Fig.104), a look that belied its acquisition and upkeep.

FIG. 103.—About 1908 a craze for lingerie dresses, particularly white ones, emerged. These dresses recorded beautiful workmanship on airy fabrics. Two examples shown here are Art Embroidery combined with multiple varieties of lace on fine white lawn (left) and a simpler version with many tucks and insertions of Valenciennes lace with batiste dress (right).

These sparkling white gowns and waists were worn by women and girls from every walk of life for all sorts of occasions; rural settings were no exception. Treatises appeared on "The Art of Wearing White," and magazines had countless advertisements for white lingerie dresses. Bellas Hess and Co. of New York, F. H. Macy, Siegel Cooper of Chicago, Philipsborn, The Outer Garment

Fig. 104.—Leisure hours found many folks making the most of the generous porches. (Photograph from collection of The Museum, Texas Tech University.)

House, and the National Cloak and Suit Co. all offered special purchases in dainty lingerie waists and dresses of Swiss embroidery, white batiste, lingerie cloth, elaborated with insertions of Valenciennes lace, art lace, torchon, embroidered medallions, and Irish crochet in various combinations of trim. The prices ranged from $3.75 to $32.50. Lingerie shirtwaists could be had for ninety-nine cents, and some of them were available in coffee white, shell pink, or sky blue. The company that made "Linaire, the White Fabric of Quality . . . suitable for daintiest afternoon frock when combined with handsome lace and embroideries" conducted a waist contest. Thirty-four of the best waists were chosen by a jury on the basis of embroidery, fashion, and general appearance.

So popular were these beautiful dresses and so important in the wardrobe that a chronicler of the period observed that there had probably never been a greater craze for all sorts of handwork. No dress was considered complete without some dainty embroidery bearing evidence of a woman's own skillful fingers and good taste. Any available time could well be taken up with this needlework. Many of these dresses reflected a great deal of creativity and a combination of many varieties of lace and embroidery, and some took as long as two years for a lady to complete. The popularity of the lingerie dresses made them appropriate for weddings, graduations, Sunday wear, picnics, and even for promenades, and were a recognized necessity in every wardrobe. The light, airy dresses, still retaining a crisp freshness, abound in museums and in private collections. Dozens—no two alike—in The Museum Collection are well documented to families from over the state as well as the nation. Considering the labor of construction and unkeep, surely this look of leisure was somewhat deceptive, although nonetheless popular for all ages.

CONCLUSION

The length of time for settling Texas spanned almost 100 years and witnessed the taming of a vast, unsubdued territory. Fortified with expectation and promise, the people who came here had little else in common; yet most of them were steadfast enough to remain, and their goal became a common one. They staked their claims and became "Texians."

All the women who pioneered in Texas were not paragons of virtue, nor were they all brave, refined, and noble—neither were the men. There was a healthy cross section of personalities, nationalities, backgrounds, degrees of refinement, and goals for the future. Resulting from this congeries of humanity, however, was a state that became and has remained strong and proud.

Not many people in Texas were style setters. Fashion consciousness was low on the priority scale for most settlers. There was always a group struggling for subsistence alongside the wealthy; there were those who came by ox cart with few worldly goods, and there were those who came by stagecoach, shipping quantities of possessions. This contrast was clearly evident in their dress. However, many of the women left, in word and example, proof that they cared about themselves and their families. They cared enough to make the effort to make a decent appearance. When circumstances allowed, they kept up with what was the latest style. In other instances, they made-do with what they had—until they could have better. Remnants of the clothes that they wore speak of an intrinsic love for and need of beauty, as well as degrees of hardship, hope, and determination. Along with the actual examples of garments that remain, portraits, diaries, historical accounts, and correspondence were fitted into the jigsaw to complete the full spectrum of women's fashion on the Texas frontier.

The aim of this chronicle is to present not only a study of clothes but also an insight into the quality of the women and their way of life, spanning the broad scope of Texas' thousands of square miles through almost a full century of development. That they were not all visionaries takes nothing from the fact that they followed others' visions. That they could endure and survive and even thrive has been made evident. Texas has not become less—it is unquestionably more than the wildest early dream of its first frontier.

ACKNOWLEDGMENTS

The writer wishes to acknowledge the following persons who have assisted in abstract and concrete ways in putting together this book: Dr. Clyde Jones, Director of The Museum, Texas Tech University, whose support and confidence brought this manuscript to eventual publication; Kathy Hinson, a young staff photographer, who cheerfully met the challenges and brought much of the collection to life in photograph form; Nicky L. Olson, Museum Staff photographer, who photographed last-minute additions; Lindl Graves, friend and assistant whose diligence and untiring drive helped unravel some of the mysteries; the late Mabel D. Erwin, long-time Chairman of the Department of Clothing and Textiles at Texas Tech University, whose past guidance and motivation have been invaluable; my family—husband, Paul; daughters, Jan James and Judith Sanders-Castro; granddaughter, Jennifer; sons, John and Jeff; and daughter by marriage, Janie—who formed my best cheering squad; my adopted aunt, friend, and mentor, Mrs. Stuart C. McCarty, whose faith never faltered.

Others who deserve to be mentioned include Frances Mayhugh Holden, wife of the first Museum Director, who was instrumental in furthering the Costume Collection from its earliest inception and lent support for this goal; Dorothy Bolt, longtime, steadfast friend and fearless promoter; Pat Grappe and Maxine Blankenship, loyal volunteers who contributed with suggestions and encouragement; Bea Zeeck, Director of News and Publications for the University, and her staff, for promotion and photographing; Seymour V. Conner, for advice. Volunteers who helped in various ways to ready garments for photographing include Dr. Gene Shelden, Mrs. Harvey Dunn, and Mrs. Hoyse McMurtry, who also located some of the garments for inclusion; and Mrs. Clark Ross (Lynette) whose magic touch brought the fashion drawings to perfection.

There were University personnel as well as Museum staffers who have been supportive and helpful. They include Rose Montgomery, Museum Registrar and friend, who revived flagging spirits; Dr. J. Knox Jones, Jr., Vice President for Research and Graduate Studies of Texas Tech University, who offered encouragement and advice; Dr. Craig Black, Dr. Leslie Drew, former Directors of The Museum, who lent support in allowing study trips and in approving the project; Claudia Kidwell, Curator of Costume, Smithsonian Institution, who pointed out the uniqueness of a collection of frontier fashions and made significant suggestions; Betty Marzan Mattil and Dr. Edward Mattil, both from the Art Department, North Texas State University, who helped with invaluable background observations; Pattilou Cobb, Director of Texas Fashion Collection and loyal friend, also from North Texas State University; and Gerry Burton, Avalanche-Journal staff reporter, for various promotional backing and enthusiasm.

Specific assistance was given by Mr. W. D. Harmsen, who generously allowed the use of his Western Americana Art Collection; Mrs. Janette Long Fish for permission to reproduce her early Texas paintings by Richard Petri, "Going Visiting" and "Pioneer Cowpen"; Dr. William D. Green for the photo of his family watermelon feast; Butterick Patterns; Mr. Lor Stevenson of Montgomery Ward & Co.; and Sears, Roebuck & Co. for furnishing material on mail order service; Dr. Ralph W. Steen for reproduction rights of his *Texas News*; Deolece Parmalee for guidance to early resource materials. Judith Gibbs, young discerning friend with a sharp pencil, Dr. Selinda Sheridan, Glenell Carson, and Nina Locascio, Museum Science graduate students and assistants—all of whom willingly read proof and helped collate the index; Shirley Burgeson, who not only typed the final copy more than once, but did it with eagerness, enthusiasm, and accuracy; Elta Rouse, a personal cheering squad; and Betty Johnson, Technical Editor, with her astute observations and patient endurance. The list would not be complete without mentioning the many donors to the Museum Collection whose gifts have been used to tell this story and whose names appear at the conclusion.

Finally, the fact cannot be overlooked that as a result of the countless hours of research and composition that went into this study, there resulted the three-part full-color publication of *The Amanda Series: A Journal of Fashion History Through Paper Dolls*, published by Texas Tech Press, 1983 and 1984, which preceded this original work.

DONORS OF COSTUMES

Mrs. Emma Austin
Mr. and Mrs. Nolan Barrick
Mrs. L. T. Barron
Mrs. Floyd Beall
Dr. and Mrs. Brooks Bell
Mrs. C. B. Bentley
Mrs. Clyde A. Blakeley
Mrs. Carolyn Bosworth
Mrs. W. T. Bowser
Mrs. W. A. Boyce
Lt. Col. and Mrs. Bennett P. Browder
Mr. and Mrs. George R. Brown
Miss Eva Browning
Mrs. Ruth Bryant
Mrs. John Buesseler
Mrs. Truman Camp
Campbell Collection
Mrs. Mary Magee Cobb
Mrs. William Craig
Mrs. A. B. Cunningham
Mr. and Mrs. M. Sims Davidson
Mr. and Mrs. James DeLoache
Miss Bonnie Dysart
Mr. Earnest W. Gibson
Mrs. Jack Griggs
Mrs. J. D. Hagler
Mrs. J. M. Hall
Mrs. Julia Magee Hartley
Mrs. Lynda Hempel
Dr. and Mrs. W. C. Holden
Mrs. W. A. Hovey
Mrs. E. N. Jones
Mrs. Elizabeth Champion King
Mrs. D. S. Kritser

Dr. Mina Lamb
Mrs. George Long
Mr. and Mrs. John Lott
Mrs. W. B. McCaleb
Mrs. E. Hoyse McMurtry
Family of Sallie Reynolds Matthews
Mrs. Roger P. Mayhugh
Mrs. Helen Munnick
Mrs. Berniece Myrick
Mrs. Corinne Jowell Neely
Mrs. P. B. Penney
Mrs. Julia Leggett Pickard
Mr. and Mrs. Frank Picon
Mr. and Mrs. James Prior
Mrs. Howard Reed
Mrs. Bertha Richardson
Mr. Joe Rollo
Mrs. Harold L. Russell
Miss Dorothy Rylander
Mr. Thomas Shive
Mrs. Seaman Smith
Mrs. R. A. Studhalter
Mrs. Max Tidmore
Mrs. Joe W. Toombs
Mrs. Melvin Trail
Mrs. J. E. Vickers, Sr.
Dr. and Mrs. Joseph P. Walker
Mrs. Carl Weber
Mrs. Georgia Lee Boles Welborn
Miss Delia Wilkinson
Mrs. Roscoe Wilson
Karl Wolf Collection
Women's Council, West Texas Museum Association
Mrs. Billie Young

GLOSSARY

Albatross—Soft, lightweight woolen material with slightly creped surface; named for the bird because fabric resembles its downy breast

Armscye—Opening for a sleeve; obsolete term for armhole

Ayrshire Embroidery—Small-patterned, eyelet-type embroidery on fine muslin with needlepoint fillings

Bagatelle—A trifle, something of no importance

Balayeuse—Ruffle sewn inside bottom of woman's skirt to protect it; same as dust ruffle; French term meaning sweeper

Balloon—Sleeve cut with extreme rounded fullness from shoulder to elbow

Basque—Bodice closely fitted by seaming from shoulder to waist, with or without short skirt-like continuation

Bavolet—Ruffle that hangs down to the shoulders, added to back of bonnet

Bengaline—Corded fabric with crosswise ribbed effect; usually of silk combined with wool or cotton

Bibi bonnet—One of the many varieties of bonnets worn by women in the early nineteenth century; known also as English Cottage Bonnet, 1831-1836

Bertha—Deep collar that falls softly from bodice neckline over shoulders

Bishop sleeve—Sleeve that is full in the lower part, either loose or held by a band

Blouse—Loose-fitting garment that covers body from neck to below waist, with or without sleeves; also called "waist"

Bodice—Waist of a woman's dress; close-fitting upper part of a woman's dress

Bombazine—Lightweight fabric of silk and wool, woven in twill weave

Bretelle—Decorative suspender-like shoulder strap that extends from waistbelt in front over shoulders to waistbelt in back

Brilliantine or *Brillianteur*—Fine lustrous wool, in plain or twill weave, with cotton warp

Broché—Fabric, usually of silk, woven with a raised figure, combining plain and pile weaves

Calico—One of the earliest cotton fabrics known; perfect example of fine, plain weave; yarn-dyed, piece-dyed, or printed with patterns

"Calmender"—Slang expression referring to calendar, the process of pressing cloth through rollers to make it smooth and glossy or watered

Cassimere—Medium-weight woolen suiting cloth in twill weave, without nap; softer than worsted; may be classed as a serge with a pattern

Chatelaine—Clasp or chain upon which to hang useful or ornamental articles, such as keys, scissors; worn at waist

Chenille—Cotton, wool, silk, or rayon cord having tufted velvet-like pile protruding all around; French word for caterpillar

Cheviot—Similar to homespun wool but usually with a close-napped twill weave

Chevron—V-shaped or zigzag motif

Cisele—Type of velvet having pattern formed by contrast of cut and uncut loops; French word meaning chiseled or chased

Clair de lune—Pale greenish blue to lavender gray color; French phrase meaning moonlight

Clevis—U-shaped piece of metal with ends perforated to receive a pin; used on end of the tongue of plow, wagon, etc.

Crepe lisse—Thin, smooth, glossy silk fabric with feel of crepe; French word meaning smooth, glossy

Crepon—A crepe-weave fabric but of heavier construction.

Cuir—Beige-color with reddish cast

Cuirass—Long, tight day bodice that is boned and descends over the hips

Décolleté—Cut very low at neckline, exposing neck and back

Drab—Dull, brownish-yellow

Drummer—One who travels about soliciting customers for a wholesale dealer or jobber

Duvetyne—Cloth of cotton warp and spun silk filling; resembles compact velvet

En camien—Two colors of kindred hue

Epaulettes—Shoulder ornament to give effect of width to shoulder line

Fagotted—Thread, yarn, ribbon, braid, etc. used straight or crisscrossed in open seam to form openwork trimming

Fichu—Ruffly draping on bosom of blouse or dress

Foulard—Soft, washable, satiny silk with twill weave; usually printed design

Garibaldi waist—Shirtwaist copied from Garibaldi's shirt—high-necked, bloused, with full sleeves

Gauge—To draw in equidistant gathers by running a thread through it; used when large amount of material has to be drawn into small space

Gigot or leg-of-mutton—Sleeve that is full, loose, rounded from shoulder over elbow and fitted at wrist; having general shape of a leg of mutton

Gore—Shaped, set-in section, narrowest at the top

Grenadine—Fine, loosely woven fabric in leno weave, similar to marquisette; usually of silk or wool

Gros de Naples—Silk fabric of strong texture

Hussar blue—Term taken from the military uniform of the Hungarian cavalry

Jabot—Frill or ruffle, usually lace or lace-trimmed, worn down front of bodice and fastened at neckline

Jean—Coarse cloth of heavy weave

Jug Sleeve—Tight upper arm and puff encircling lower arm

Knickerbockers—Loose breeches banded below knees

Lappet weave—A kind of figure weaving with an extra warp or whip yarn introduced by needle attachment; makes it possible to have zigzag design on body of fabric

Madder—A herb whose root is used in dyestuff to produce turkey red color

Mantua-maker—One who makes dresses, cloaks, etc., for women

Marquisette—Soft, lightweight gauze fabric with open mesh of leno weave

Merino—Fine, wool dress fabric that resembles cashmere; originally made of the wool of merino sheep

Merveilleux—Lustrous all-silk or silk and cotton fabric woven in a twill weave

Mousseline de soie—Transparent, fine, lightweight silk that has a plain weave

Nun's veiling—Thin, soft, loosely woven woolen or silk and woolen fabric that has a plain weave

Ottoman—Heavy, luxurious fabric with broad, flat crosswise ribs, usually silk or wool

Pagoda sleeve—Sleeve large at bottom, fitted at the armhole; adopted from formal costume of the Chinese

Passementerie—Trimmings, especially heavy embroideries or edgings, of rich gimps, braid, beads, silk, tinsel, etc.

Pelerine—Waist-length tippet or cape with pointed ends in front

Pintadores—Painted, marked, or stamped using stamp of clay or stone

Plait—Variant of pleat, a fold of fabric laid back flat

Poke Bonnet—Bonnet with rounded front brim, small crown at back

Polonaise—Term used for dress with bodice and looped-up tunic; named after Polish national costume

Pompadour print—Silk fabric with figures of flowers or bouquets

Pouter pigeon—Term applied to puffed-out effect at the breast that resembles inflated crop of pouter pigeons

Primrose—Bright, clear, delicate yellow color

Puncheon—A split log or heavy slab with the face smoothed

Quilling—Band of quilled material composed of rounded ridges resembling rows of quills; also one of the fluting or folds so made

Reseda—French word meaning mignonette; term applied to a grayish green color that resembles the color of the flower

Rouleau—Roll or fold of ribbon, as for piping

Selvage—Lengthwise edge of woven fabric, finished so it will not ravel

Serpentine—Braid that winds or turns one way and then the other

Silesia—Strong, lightweight twilled cotton fabric used for linings

Solferino—Color with bluish red hue; so called for the battle of 1859 in Solferino, Italy

Spermaceti—A white, waxy solid that separates from the oil obtained from the sperm whale

Sphynx gray—Deep stone hue

Sutler—One who follows the army and sells provisions to the troops; early-day term for storekeeper

Tarlatan—Thin, open-mesh, transparent muslin that is slightly stiffened

Thibet superfine—Wool material, worsted with soft and smooth plain-finished face; made from mountain sheep of Thibet, Asia

Toilette—Attire, especially fashionable attire; term for woman's entire costume

Val or Valenciennes lace—Flat bobbin lace worked in one piece with the same thread forming both the ground and the design; also narrow machine-made lace used for lingerie and wash dresses

Wadded—Formed into a pad; stuffed or lined with padding

Waist—Garment or part of garment covering body from shoulders to waistline; usually called blouse or bodice

Watteau—Having certain features seen in costume painted by French eighteenth-century artist Antoine Watteau; back of gown with fullness taken up in box plait from neck to waistline, hanging loosely from shoulders

Wool plant—Early reference to cotton

Wrapper—Loose, informal garment for casual wear; often belted

Zanella cloth—Closely woven, twilled fabric of silk and worsted; also called gloria

Zephyr—Thin, fine cassimere or lightweight worsted wool; name is from Zephyrus, classical god of the wind

LITERATURE CITED

The Albany News (Shackelford County, Texas), 20 September 1901.

Arthur's Home Magazine, 1874, 1887, 1899.

American Fabrics Magazine. 1960. *Encyclopedia of textiles*. Englewood Cliffs: Prentice-Hall.

Arnold, J. 1972. *Patterns of fashion I: 1660-1860*. New York: Drama Book Specialists.

Barr, A. E. 1913. *All the days of my life: an autobiography*. New York: D. Appleton & Co.

Barton, H. T. 1928. A history of the J A Ranch. *Southwestern Historical Quarterly*, 21:227.

Beecher, C. E. 1849. *A treatise of domestic economy*. New York: Harper & Bros.

Beecher, C. E. and H. B. Stowe. 1869. *The American woman's home*. New York: J. B. Ford & Co.

Bracht, V. 1931. *Texas in 1848*. Translated by C. F. Schmidt. San Antonio: Naylor Printing Co.

Brown, D. 1972. *The gentle tamers: women of the old wild west*. Lincoln: Univ. of Nebraska Press.

Carl, P. 1937. *Texas 1844-1845*. Translated from German. Houston: Anson Jones Press.

Carrington, E. M., ed. 1975. *Women in early Texas*. Austin: Jenkins Publishing Co., The Pemberton Press.

Carrow, C. I. 1947. Amusements for men and women in Texas in the 1880's. *West Texas Historical Association Year Book*, 23:77-85.

Chabot, F. C., ed. 1940. *Texas letters*. San Antonio: Yanaguana Society.

Clark, T. D. 1964. *Pills, petticoats, and plows*. Norman: Univ. of Oklahoma Press.

Cleaveland, A. M. 1941. *No life for a lady*. Cambridge, Mass.: The Riverside Press.

Connor, S. V., ed. 1958. *The reminiscences of Mary A. Blankenship*. Lubbock: West Texas Museum Assoc.

The Cosmopolitan, 1890.

Crosby County News (Estacado, Texas), 28 November 1889.

Cunnington, C. W., P. Cunnington, and C. Beard. 1976. *A dictionary of English costume*. London: Adam & Charles Black.

Davis, M. J. 1974. *Early American embroidery designs*. New York: Crown Publishers.

The Delineator, 1891, 1901, 1902, 1907.

Dewees, W. B. *Letters from an early settler of Texas*. Reprint of 1852 edition. Waco: Texian Press, 1968.

Fisher, O. 1940. *Sketches of Texas in 1840*. Reprint of 1840 edition. Waco: Texian Press.

Godey's Lady's Book and Magazine, 1840, 1865, 1870, 1875.

Green, B. 1974. *The dancing was lively*. San Angelo, Tex.: Ft. Concho Sketches Publishing Co.

Groves, S. 1973. *The history of needlework tools and accessories*. New York: Arco Publishing Co.

Harland, M. 1886. *Common sense in the household*. New York: Charles Scribner's Sons.

Harper's Bazar, 1870, 1874, 1903, 1904, 1905.

Hart, K., and E. Kemp, eds. 1974. *Lucadia Pease and the Governor; letters: 1850-1857*. Austin: Encino Press.

Hogan, W. R. 1947. *The Texas Republic*. Norman: Univ. of Oklahoma Press.

Holden, W. C. 1930. *Alkali trails or social and economic movements on the Texas frontier: 1846-1900*. Dallas: Southwest Press.

Holley, M. A. 1836. *Texas*. Lexington, Kent.: J. Clarke & Co.

Home and Farm (Louisville, Kentucky), 1 January 1895.

The Houston Post, April 1885.

The Industrial Advantages of Houston, Texas and Environs. 1894. Houston, Texas: The Akerhurst Publishing Co.

Kerr, R. N. 1951. *100 years of costumes in America*. Worcester, Mass.: Davis Press.

Kidwell, C. B. 1979. *Cutting a fashionable fit*. Washington, D.C.: Smithsonian Institution Press.

Kidwell, C. B., and M. C. Christman. 1974. *Suiting everyone: the democratization of clothing in America*. Washington, D.C.: Smithsonian Institution Press.

The Ladies' World, 1909.

Lantz, L. K. 1970. *Old American kitchenware: 1725-1925.* Camden, N.Y.: Thomas Nelson Inc. and Everybody's Press.

Lee, R. S. 1962. *Mary Austin Holley.* Austin: Univ. of Texas Press.

Lubbock, F. R. 1900. *Six decades in Texas.* Austin: Ben C. Jones & Co.

Lubbock Leader (Texas), 31 July 1891.

McCall's Magazine, 1906.

Mme. Demorest's Quarterly Mirror of Fashion, 1861, 1864.

Mason County News, 2 November 1889; 5 January 1895.

Matthews, S. R. 1958. *Interwoven.* 3rd ed. Austin: Univ. of Texas Press.

New York Fashion Bazar, 1889.

Payne, B. 1965. *History of costume.* New York: Harper & Row Publishers.

Pennybacker, A. J. H. 1888. *A new history of Texas.* Privately printed.

Peterson's Magazine, 1864, 1865, 1871, 1878, 1881, 1887.

Pickrell, A. D. 1970. *Pioneer women in Texas.* Austin & N.Y.: Jenkins Publishing Co., The Pemberton Press.

Ragsdale, C. S., ed. 1976. *The golden free land: the reminiscences and letters of women on an American frontier.* Austin: Landmark Press.

Reid, M. 1942. Fashion of the Republic. *The Southwestern Historical Quarterly,* 45:246-250.

Roberts, Mrs. D. W. n.d. *A woman's reminiscences of six years in camp with the Texas Rangers.* Austin: Press of Von Boeckmann-Jones Co.

The San Antonio Express and News, 25 October 1867; 1 October 1899.

Schmitz, J. W. 1960. *Texas culture in the days of the Republic.* San Antonio: Naylor Co.

Spikes, N. W., and T. A. Ellis. 1952. Entries in general store day book in Old Emma. Pp. 289-294 in *Through the years: a history of Crosby County, Texas.* San Antonio: Naylor Co.

Steen, R. W., ed. 1955. *The Texas news.* Austin: Steck Co.

The Stockman (Colorado City, Texas), 21 June 1900.

Walker, O. T. 1944. Esther Amanda Sherrill Cullins. *Southwestern Historical Quarterly,* 47:234-249.

The Weekly Review (Sweetwater, Texas), 1900.

INDEX